WORD BOOK

die Auferstehung (Resurrection)

WORD BOOK

LUDWIG WITTGENSTEIN

Translated by Bettina Funcke
Critical Introduction by Désirée Weber
Art by Paul Chan

With additional translation by
Nickolas Calabrese, Catherine Schelbert
& Désirée Weber

New York

Word Book
by Ludwig Wittgenstein
2020

First printing (during the 2020 covid global pandemic)

Published by Badlands Unlimited LLC. with
Badlands Institute for Art & Social Research Inc.

Very special thanks to Eleanor Cayre

Special thanks to Carol Greene, Jeffrey Rowledge, Martha Fleming-Ives
and the rest of the staff at Greene Naftali Gallery

Editor: Paul Chan
Assistant editor: Nickolas Calabrese
Translation advisor: Désirée Weber, Catherine Schelbert
Copyeditor: James Yeh
Book designer: Paul Chan

Paper book distributed in the Americas by:
ARTBOOK | D.A.P.
75 Broad Street, Suite 630
New York, NY 10004
www.artbook.com

Paper book distributed in Europe by:
Buchhandlung Walther König
Ehrenstrasse 4
50672 Köln
www.buchhandlung-walther-koenig.de

Printed in the United States of America

ISBN: 978-1-943263-24-0

Badlands Unlimited LLC.
Badlands Institute for Art & Social Research Inc.

CONTENTS

die Auskunft, Auskünfte (information)

LIST OF ARTWORKS

das Edelweiß (edelweiss)

CRITICAL INTRODUCTION
Désirée Weber

In the spring of 1923, fourth-grade student Leopoldine Eichberger was practicing her grammar lessons and noting which words were giving her trouble under the watchful eye and strict guidance of her elementary school teacher, Ludwig Wittgenstein. She was one of many primary school pupils that Wittgenstein taught between 1920 and 1926 in a series of small villages in Austria. The years when this influential philosopher dedicated himself to teaching young pupils are not well understood—and the dictionary that he authored during this time even less so.

For six years, Wittgenstein instructed the children of farmers and factory workers in the rural communities of Trattenbach, Puchberg am Schneeberg, and Otterthal in Lower Austria. He was responsible for teaching students in grades four through six all subjects, from writing to mathematics, science to music. His service in World War I and his long struggle to publish the *Tractatus Logico-Philosophicus*—a work he considered to be a conclusive answer to the extant questions of philosophy—had alienated him from academic philosophy. Having grown up in one of the wealthiest families in Europe, he had renounced his significant inheritance a few years earlier: he sought an ascetic life. His self-imposed exile from the world of philosophy and Cambridge (where Wittgenstein studied and taught before and after this period) thus rendered his years as a schoolteacher an "entirely rural affair."[1]

Throughout 1925, he worked on putting together a small dictionary of German words for his students, which would become known as the *Wör-*

---

1   Ray Monk, *Ludwig Wittgenstein: The Duty of Genius* (London: Vintage, 1990), 192.

terbuch für Volksschulen (Dictionary for Elementary Schools). It was published by a Viennese press in the fall of 1926. This was a few months after a harrowing corporal punishment incident in which Wittgenstein struck a student, causing the student to collapse. He abruptly abandoned his teaching career and moved back to Vienna. The dictionary Wittgenstein produced would become the second of only two works that was published in his lifetime. The original volume of forty-two pages and nearly six thousand word entries was meant to fill a pedagogic need for his students. The two dictionaries available at the time were not up to the task: "[o]ne was too big and too expensive to be used by children . . . . [t]he other was too small and badly put together, containing many foreign words which the children were unlikely ever to use, and omitting many words commonly misspelt by children."[2]

However, as one of the most eminent philosophical thinkers of the twentieth century, he could not leave behind his insatiable fascination with language and meaning in his new career. Beyond practical needs, Wittgenstein's keen interest in how his students were learning the use of words and their spelling becomes clear through his justifications and explanations provided in the dictionary's preface. His meticulous choices and attention to detail in how to construct the book helped to "guard [the student] against confusions in the best way possible."[3] How does a young student learn a new word, idea, or concept when previously they were unable to use it themselves? An adult can often rely on prior concepts in relation to which a new concept makes sense, but a child learning a word or concept for the first time often does not have such prior understanding to bring to bear on a new idea. Instead, a child needs to practice and have the chance to use the word in new contexts. This lesson stuck with Wittgenstein many years later, when he wrote that "the usefulness of this sign must emerge from *experience*."[4] And the dictionary was a means for his students to gain just that.

Wittgenstein's understanding of how children learn to use language through experience relies in turn on his experiences teaching them to use language in the first place. This process of teaching and learning—a com-

---

2   Ibid., 225–26. On this point, see also Wittgenstein, "Word Book: A Preface," in this volume.

3   Wittgenstein, "Word Book: A Preface," in this volume, 29.

4   Ludwig Wittgenstein, *On Certainty*, ed. G. E. M. Anscombe and G. H. von Wright, trans. Denis Paul and G. E. M. Anscombe (New York: Harper Torchbooks, 1969), §575 (emphasis in original).

plex interaction between ourselves and others—is central to being able to create and understand meaning. The ability to communicate also requires established patterns of meaning and the possibility of *trusting* in that shared meaning—in its certainty and solidity, its repeatability and shared character. This complex interaction of meaning, practices, and language use that we are all brought into is the same process that allows us to be certain about anything at all. As Wittgenstein explains, the phrase "'[w]e are quite sure of it' does not mean just that every single person is certain of it, but that we belong to a community which is bound together by science and education."[5] It is the community of language speakers which participates in using language that at once reaffirms what is understood as certain and in so doing functions as the fragile guarantor of community itself.

This contextual, intersubjective understanding of how meaning functions—and indeed Wittgenstein's experience with teaching young students—is at the heart of his later thinking. In the *Philosophical Investigations*, the major work of his later period, Wittgenstein examines how language works despite its not resting on any universal foundations or certain referents that could be thought to underwrite meaning as such.[6] And in so doing, he returns again and again to examples involving students because they illustrate the complex, iterative, and communal ways in which meaning is established and used. This is a departure from his pre-1920s thinking, where his method for discovering how language relates to the world was austere, axiomatic, and couched in the structures of logical formalism.

In this light, the *Wörterbuch* is not just an artifact of Wittgenstein's time as a teacher, but one that gives insight into his thinking about language during the years in which he had all but given up doing philosophy as a vocation. His new professional obligations as a teacher and his long-standing scholarly interests in how the uses of language intertwine with our forms of life are themselves interwoven in this slim volume.

The Dictionary's Language and Its Community

Within the pages of the word list, the students in Wittgenstein's classroom coalesce into a community of language learners at the same time as they also

---

5   Ibid., §298.
6   The *Philosophical Investigations* was published posthumously in 1953 but is the culmination of work Wittgenstein began as early as the 1930s.

become part of the wider community of Austrian and other German-speaking language users. In a letter to his editor that later became the preface to the work, he explained that he excluded most foreign words and included colloquial and dialect-based words commonly used in rural Austria. He followed several principles for the selection of words: "Only those words that students of Austrian elementary schools are familiar with should be included in the word book."[7] Additionally, any foreign words that were included "should be . . . translated into German if this is not too difficult."[8] Wittgenstein's decisions about which words to include anticipate in detail how his students' specific language use would best be aided by the dictionary.

Wittgenstein took care to include words that were appropriate not only to the grade level but also to the geographic region in which he was teaching and the particular use of words in the regional dialect of Lower Austria. For the most part, he left out more advanced words, as well as some words used primarily in Germany that were not prevalent in rural Austria.[9] Wittgenstein included many words that relate to the alpine terrain, common occupations in the region at that time, and colloquial descriptions of people (even insults). For example, he included words like *Sennerin* (alpine shepherdess), which not only reflects a typical, geographically specific occupation, but is also a word used specifically in Austria that is rare in other German-speaking areas.[10] Similar examples of such words, specifically *Ribisel* (red currant) instead of *Johannisbeere*[11] and *bähen* (baking or toasting) instead of *backen*.[12]

At times, Wittgenstein also included the regional or dialect variation in addition to the standard German, such as the entry for the word *squir-*

---

7   Wittgenstein, "Word Book: A Preface," in this volume, 27.

8   Ibid., 28.

9   For a fuller description, see my article "Lessons about Language in Wittgenstein's *Dictionary for Elementary Schools*" on which the present analysis is based.

10 Ludwig Wittgenstein, *Wörterbuch für Volksschulen* (Vienna: Hölder-Pichler-Tempsky, 1926), 33 (my own translation). This word has many regional and dialect-based variations in the German-speaking regions of Austria. In Kärnten, *Prentler* and *Almhatler* are used, while in Switzerland the term is *Älpler*. In German-speaking parts of Italy and particular areas of Germany like Bavaria, the preferred term is *Halter*. See entry for "Prentler, Brentler," *Das österreichische Volkswörterbuch*, October 10, 2011, https://www.ostarrichi.org/wort/18967/Prentler_Brentler. See also Michael Jungmeier and Judith Drapela, *Almen, Nationalpark Hohe Tauern* (Matrei in Osttirol: Wissenschaftliche Schriften, 2004), 60–64.

11 Wittgenstein, *Wörterbuch für Volksschulen*, 28 (my own translation).

12 Ibid., 3 (my own translation).

rel, which reads: "das Eichhörnchen, Eichkätzchen."[13] The meaning of some words in the dictionary is elucidated with reference to more idiomatic expressions and how the word would have been used in the regional dialect. Wittgenstein uses pertinent examples, instead of just the proper definition or grammar rules, to elucidate the use and meaning of words for his students.

Some words that Wittgenstein included illustrate his attention and sensitivity to the regional context of a word's usage in a different way: they indicate specific habits or social practices that were common at the time in rural Austria but few other places. One of those entries is *Schnaderhüpfel*,[14] an improvised spoken word performance that consists of at least two singers or speakers who take turns exchanging four-line stanzas. The lines are addressed from one performer to another and are often celebratory, comical, or insulting. These exchanges, set to well-known musical refrains and performed at gatherings or celebrations, have been analogized to the Alpine version of rap battles—and are a resurgent cultural form in Austria today.[15] Wittgenstein thus captured not only the specificity of the rural Austrian dialect with which his students were familiar, but also a sense of the words that pertained to their community's cultural lexicon.

Wittgenstein carefully prepared his students to enter into the community of language as active participants. He emphasized learning through direct experience, taking responsibility, and honing their judgment in creating and discerning meaning. Instead of having students simply memorize words and their usage as though they were akin to multiplication tables, Wittgenstein insisted that students needed to build up their familiarity and make correct inferences about the relationships between words and meanings for themselves. He connected this pedagogic need to the volume he published: "Only a word book makes it possible to hold the student responsible... because it provides them with a reliable tool for finding and correcting their mistakes.... It is absolutely necessary that the student can correct their own mistakes. They should feel confident that they are the only author of

---

13 Ibid., 7 (my own translation). The direct translation for *Eichkätzchen* is oak kitten.

14 Ibid., 31 (my own translation). See also Gerlinde Haid, "Gstanzl," in Band 2, *Österreichisches Musiklexikon* (Vienna: Verlag der Österreichischen Akademie der Wissenschaften, 2003).

15 Doris Wild, "Rap trifft Gstanzl beim Red Bull Gstanzl Battle," *Salzburgerland Magazin*, November 15, 2017, https://www.salzburgerland.com/de/magazin/rap-trifft-gstanzl-im-red-bull-battle/.

their work and they alone ought to be responsible for it."[16] One's authorship in using language and participating in the wider play of meaning in a community thus comes from the learned responsibility and judgment that experience with a language and its culturally contextual meanings furnish.

Experience, Certainty, and Aesthetic Judgment

We make and inhabit worlds of meaning through language. How we learn to use language, what experiences we gather, and which linguistic practices we are a part of shapes our path through those worlds—indeed it shapes our very understanding of those worlds. Experience also helps us to develop our judgments about which concepts make sense and which do not, which we accept and which we reject.

The experiences with and in language that we gather are an important part of how we learn the patterns of meaning and forms of life that Wittgenstein calls language-games. And yet experience, like mere exposure and rote training, is not enough to allow us to effectively navigate the complex world of meaning. The creativity of language and the flexibility of meaning cannot be explained adequately if words are thought to have just one fixed, unambiguous, objective meaning that we can memorize. The challenge of how to make sense of this complex notion of meaning is heightened when we are disabused of the idea that we can presume the existence of stable, universal referents that undergird meaning, as Wittgenstein teaches us. Try as we might, we do not have direct access to a "beyond" or "behind" or "underneath"—a firmament or transcendental realm (if such a thing were to exist)—that can provide certain foundations for meaning. But at the same time, we are not thrown forever adrift on the sea of meaning: it is a fact that we *do* make sense of and to each other. This contingent stability of meaning that we create *between us* requires that we are able to make judgements about a variety of experiences and meanings, not all of which are commensurable with each other. How do we determine what is sense and what nonsense?

The philosopher Stanley Cavell captures the beauty but also the precarity of this conception of language: "We learn and teach words in certain contexts. . . . Nothing insures that this will take place. . . . That on the whole we *do* is a matter of our sharing routes of interest and feeling, modes of response, senses of humor and of significance and of fulfillment, of what is outrageous, of what is similar to what else, what a rebuke, what forgiveness,

---

16 Wittgenstein, "Word Book: A Preface," in this volume, 25.

of when an utterance is an assertion, when an appeal, when an explanation—all the whirl of organism Wittgenstein calls 'forms of life.' Human speech and activity, sanity and community, rest upon nothing more, but nothing less, than this."[17]

Language and meaning, in Wittgenstein's philosophical work after his experience teaching kids, do not rest on universal referents or immutable foundations, whether in the world or within our minds: meaning accrues in the use of language between us. And it does so over time and in the midst of efforts by all those who belong to the community of language users. This complex interweaving means that "[t]o understand the various uses of a word is to know not only that word but a considerable part of the language that uses the word, and thus to participate in the cultural conditions of that language."[18]

What results is an intricate, non-reductive conception of language, where meaning is contingently stable—able to be relied upon but also flexible to change—and suspended between us language users. Meaning is neither under an individual's sole control, nor only determined by the majority of speakers. Hanna Pitkin explains the contours and advantages of Wittgenstein's vision of language which navigates between a handful of intertwined traditional philosophical dualities: "On the one hand, Wittgenstein seems to stress nominalistic, individualistic . . . themes: each child learns and interprets language regularities for himself; any rule or principle needs to be interpreted; words must always be capable of projection into new and unexpected contexts; concepts are fragmented and often their grammar has inconsistent implications; and since what is 'in the world' depends very much on our concepts, the world itself shares these qualities." But Wittgenstein does not simply reject the positions that would be diametrically opposite either. He "stress[es] that there are mistakes in using language; that words do have meaning that can be looked up in a good dictionary; that not just any new projection of a concept will be acceptable; that not just any excuse will be appropriate; that we can't say just anything at any time and in any context; that it is not merely up to each individual what his words mean; and that in a significant sense we all live in the same, continuing, objective world, and our real activity in that world is what

17 Stanley Cavell, *Must We Mean What We Say?* (Cambridge: Cambridge University Press, 2002), 52 (emphasis added).
18 Kennan Ferguson, *The Politics of Judgment: Aesthetics, Identity, and Political Theory* (Lanham: Lexington Books, 1999) 19–20.

underlies and shapes our concepts."[19]

Wittgenstein's later philosophy avoids the slippery slope of relativism without resorting to a static conception of language. He interweaves our individual and collective roles in language. As he puts it: "If language is to be a means of communication there must be agreement not only in definitions but also . . . in judgments."[20] The process of learning judgments, then, comes centrally into focus in Wittgenstein's thought. Navigating the worlds of meaning in which we find ourselves requires a keen sense of judgment, especially without recourse to stable referents and when no objective criteria for evaluating ultimate meaning are available. The need and necessity of rendering judgment without universal metrics to rely on is akin to aesthetic judgment. The creation of art and our subsequent assessments of it do not ultimately rest on universally applicable standards or ways of discernment.

Understanding which aesthetic experiences we find beautiful or abhorrent, which ones strike us as awesome or mundane, is a similar challenge as understanding which words we find meaningful or nonsensical, which ones strike us as profound or trite. Kennan Ferguson shows the affinities between Wittgenstein's thinking on language and aesthetic judgment: one central characteristic of judgment following a Wittgensteinian line is that "judgments are always and only located in particular kinds of experiences. . . . [They are] specific not only to what is being judged but who is doing the judging."[21] There is an intrinsic plurality to judging and judgments that moves us even further away from the assumption that judgment is about discovering one absolutely right conclusion that can hold for all instances.

One's ability to generate meaning and the relationship between oneself and another is thus central to Wittgenstein's thinking. His own experience with teaching aided his thinking about philosophical issues when he returned to Cambridge and his experience as a schoolteacher honed his judgment in his later work, just as our experiences shape our own judgments and what makes sense to us. The dictionary he wrote is thus emblematic of Wittgenstein's later philosophy of language and the complexities of meaning.

---

19 Hanna Pitkin, *Wittgenstein and Justice: On the Significance of Ludwig Wittgenstein for Social and Political Thought* (Berkeley: University of California Press, 1972), 194.

20 Wittgenstein, *Philosophical Investigations*, §242.

21 Ferguson, *The Politics of Judgment: Aesthetics, Identity, and Political Theory*, 17.

Bibliography

Cavell, Stanley. *Must We Mean What We Say?* Cambridge: Cambridge University Press, 2002.

Ferguson, Kennan. *The Politics of Judgment: Aesthetics, Identity, and Political Theory.* Lanham: Lexington Books, 1999.

Haid, Gerlinde. "Gstanzl." In Band 2, *Oesterreichisches Musiklexikon.* Vienna: Verlag der Österreichischen Akademie der Wissenschaften, 2003.

Jungmeier, Michael, and Judith Drapela. *Almen, Nationalpark Hohe Tauern.* Matrei in Osttirol: Wissenschaftliche Schriften, 2004.

Monk, Ray. *Ludwig Wittgenstein: The Duty of Genius.* London: Vintage, 1990.

Pitkin, Hanna Fenichel. *Wittgenstein and Justice: On the Significance of Ludwig Wittgenstein for Social and Political Thought.* Berkeley: University of California Press, 1972.

Wild, Doris. "Rap trifft Gstanzl beim Red Bull Gstanzl Battle." *Salzburgerland Magazin.* November 15, 2017. https://www.salzburgerland.com/de/magazin/rap-trifft-gstanzl-im-red-bull-battle/.

Wittgenstein, Ludwig. *On Certainty.* Edited by G. E. M. Anscombe and G. H. von Wright. Translated by Denis Paul and G. E. M. Anscombe. New York: Harper Torchbooks, 1969.

———. *Philosophische Untersuchungen/Philosophical Investigations: The German Text, with a Revised English Translation*, 3rd ed. Translated by G. E. M. Anscombe. Malden, MA: Blackwell Publishing, 2001.

———. "Preface." In *Wörterbuch für Volksschulen.* Edited by Adolf Hübner, Werner Leinfellner, and Elisabeth Leinfellner. Translated by Elisabeth Leinfellner. Vienna: Hölder-Pichler-Tempsky, 1977.

———. *Tractatus Logico-Philosophicus.* New York/London: Routledge, 1922.

———. *Wörterbuch für Volksschulen.* Vienna: Hölder-Pichler-Tempsky, 1926.

References for Further Reading

Norval, Aletta J. "Democratic Identification: A Wittgensteinian Approach." *Political Theory* 34, no. 2 (2006): 229–55.

Peters, Michael A., Nicholas C. Burbules, and Paul Smeyers. *Showing and Doing: Wittgenstein as a Pedagogical Philosopher.* Boulder, CO: Paradigm Publishers, 2010.

Wittgenstein, Ludwig. *The Blue and Brown Books: Preliminary Studies for the 'Philosophical Investigations'.* Edited by Rush Rhees. New York: Harper Torchbooks, 1960.

Wünsche, Konrad. *Der Volksschullehrer Ludwig Wittgenstein.* Frankfurt am Main: Suhrkamp Verlag, 1985.

TRANSLATOR'S PREFACE
Bettina Funcke

Recently I found myself wondering about the history of standardized spelling. Did it come about because, after the chaos of the Hundred Years' War, Europe needed order and clarity? Or was it more complex? These reflections arose while leafing through Ludwig Wittgenstein's almost century-old *Wörterbuch für Volksschulen* (translated for this publication as *Word Book*). Whenever we articulate a thought, feeling, or experience in words, we find that language itself has a way of abstracting things. Here we approach the concerns of Wittgenstein himself: how does one express something in a precise manner?

I am neither a professional translator nor a Wittgenstein scholar, but maybe this is why Paul Chan invited me to translate the philosopher's as-yet-untranslated dictionary into English. Maybe Paul trusted my German upbringing and my philosophical education in Karlsruhe. Maybe he appreciated that I have a young daughter who keeps me in touch with the idiosyncrasies of English orthography and the challenge of learning to spell correctly.

It was immediately clear to me that we should make this a bilingual *Word Book*, preserving the German so as to retain the alphabetical order, as well as keeping a sense of Wittgenstein's original purpose. Printing entries in both German and English also makes visible the riches that arise from the gaps between the languages. The structure of German allows for many possible translations, particularly in the case of prepositions and verbs, and for the first months of work my game was weeding out different translations for any given word. The German language often allows for a literal, figurative meaning as well as an abstraction, and the two senses are often deeply connected to each other, as with *der Abzug* (deduction, withdrawal, and contact print), *die Zerstreuung* (absentmindedness and dispersion), and *das Wesen* (a being and a soul). A word can be both adjective and verb, such as *überlegen* (superior, and to reflect). One of my favorites is *Sorge* (care, and worry). This double meaning of *Sorge* guided me as I weighed the various word options and their sliding meanings, most often dependent on context or the certain way a word was used.

Having decided on a particular range of translations, it was an equally difficult challenge to determine the order in which to place them. Considering the many discrepancies between English and German, the different possible translations are listed next to each other, in an attempted order of relevance.

In addition to the *Duden*, the authoritative German dictionary, I used websites on Austrian dialect, lists of name analogues (*Wilhelm*/William, *Susanne*/Susan), and three online dictionaries: Langenscheidt, the classic German dual-language dictionary; Leo, initiated by the computer science department of the Technical University of Munich, and Beolingus, maintained by the Chemnitz University of Technology (I was introduced to these tools by my late friend the translator and philologist Warren Niesluchowski; his preference was Beo). The variety of translations the three sources supplied was astonishing, and they all possess different approaches to meaning, grammar, and context. Of the three, Langenscheidt is solidly based in current usage, and is the most user-friendly. The others were founded in academic contexts, which yield more historical word choices. Beo's strength lies in displaying varieties of linguistic context. While it was not my first choice for proper translation, it was often the only source for the many strange words I was dealing with. After all, I was translating a nearly hundred-year-old book made with and for children, full of words that were archaic, or grounded in Austrian dialect, or referring to then-familiar childhood activities. Sometimes these were words I hadn't heard since my own childhood.

While translating, I made groupings to keep track of words. These groupings indicate Wittgenstein's philosophical interests of the time, as much as his schoolchildren's world: engineering and architecture, mathematics, local slang and practices, concrete terms from life (tools, food, the home, health), nature (including animals and plants), farming, school work (language, writing, math, geography, music), religion, professions, and first names.

I want to mention that before any linguistic translation could begin, the *Word Book* had to go through a more figurative translation between different media and formats. Paul had found a copy of the original *Wörterbuch*, and the first question was how to turn this object into a workable computer file. The book had been printed in the archaic blackletter typeface Fraktur, which Paul explained was too idiosyncratic to run through commercial software that automatically turns printed language into editable text. The calligraphic lines of the typeface are broken into many angles, unlike smoother modern typefaces. His studio scanned the book and mailed me a stapled printout in an envelope, old-style. Long-ago Latin study had left me only somewhat familiar with Fraktur, and the small and relatively faint printout made the letters difficult to decipher. Even under a magnifying glass the *s* looked like an *f*, *tz* read as *ft* or *ß*, *ck* resembled a *d*, and so on.

Fraktur

Luckily, artist's studios turn out to contain myriad talents. In our case, Nickolas Calabrese, a tattooed Wittgensteinian, artist, and computer specialist put in some weeks of work. Eventually he was able to send me a compressed folder containing 126 PNG files and 126 TXT files. The PNG files were images of each of the *Word Book's* 126 vocabulary columns; the TXT files contained algorithmically translated scans of the columns, from image to text. The next move was to merge the 126 TXT files into a single Word document, which I did, carefully copying and pasting them in alphabetical order. I then corrected mistakes due to the transfer process; these cropped up frequently, perhaps every other word. If a word was scrambled beyond recognition, I was able to compare it to the PNG scan and manually correct it.

Wittgenstein could not have dreamed of such twenty-first-century formatting questions when he dictated word lists to his students in a classroom in the foothills of the Austrian Alps. He was entirely dependent on what in German is called *Schönschrift*: the students' best, most readable handwriting. The story of exactly how these dictated and handwritten documents were transformed into a typeset volume and published by Hölder-Pichler-Tempsky is a relatively unexplored chapter in Wittgenstein scholarship. As

Désirée Weber writes in her critical introduction to the *Word Book*: "This contextual, intersubjective understanding of how meaning functions—and indeed Wittgenstein's experience with teaching young students—is at the heart of his later thinking. . . . In this light, the *Wörterbuch* is not just an artifact of Wittgenstein's time as a teacher, but one that gives insight into his thinking about language during the years that he had all but given up doing philosophy as vocation. His new professional obligations as a teacher and his long-standing scholarly interests in how the uses of language intertwine with our forms of life are themselves interwoven in this slim volume."

The right way to spell will always be up for discussion. Over the course of the last century, many of the German spellings themselves have changed, but I didn't correct any of these; in this sense the *Word Book* remains a representation of Wittgenstein's era. My choices of English translation, however, may never fully settle, and this is as it should be: maintaining balance implies not stasis but constant slight movement, back and forth. This brings me back to my reflections on the history of spelling. Prior to the mid-seventeenth century, when dictionaries were introduced, people had simply sounded out words anew every time they wished to write them. Then the English spelling system began to stabilize, during a period of absolutist ideas that Thomas Hobbes articulated in his book *Leviathan*, whose well-known frontispiece depicts a monarch hovering over his land, his own form composed of the many bodies of his people. In this image it is possible to see a dictionary that holds all words, arranged according to the alphabet, the letters of each word assembled in the right order, and it's all in your hands.

—New York, October 2019

der Geist, geistig (spirit, spiritual)

die Pflege, pflegen, der Pfleger (care, to take care, caretaker)

WORD BOOK: A PREFACE
Ludwig Wittgenstein

The goal of this word book is to fill an urgent need with respect to how orthography is presently taught. It is a result of the author's practical experience: In order to improve correct spelling in his class and, in order to enable students to inform themselves about the spelling of a word, the author found it necessary to supply them with word books. First, such a word book should enable the student to look up a word as quickly as possible; and second, the way in which the word book guides the student should enable them to remember the looked-up word permanently. The spelling of words becomes an interesting and urgent problem for the student primarily when it comes to improving their compositional writing. But the frequent questioning of the teacher, or of fellow classmates, distracts the other students in their work. This questioning of classmates and teacher also encourages a certain mental sluggishness. Furthermore, the student is often given the wrong information from their classmates. Moreover, information that is spoken leaves a far weaker imprint on the memory than that which has been read. Only a word book makes it possible to hold the student responsible for the spelling of what they have written because it provides them with a reliable tool for finding and correcting their mistakes, granted that they are inclined to do so. It is absolutely necessary that the student can correct their own mistakes. They should feel confident that they are the only author of their work and they alone ought to be responsible for it. This independence is also what allows the teacher to get a fuller picture of the student's knowledge and their mental capacities. The exchange of workbooks and the reciprocal correction of compositions results in a distorted image, so to speak, of the class' abilities. From the work of student A, I do not want to at the same time find out what student B knows. I want to learn what student B knows from student B's work. And this reciprocal correction does not even—as is sometimes claimed—give an accurate picture of the class' general level. (This would only be true if each student corrected the writing of all of their classmates, which, naturally, is impossible). I also believe that the teacher should not be invested in such general spelling; it is not *the class* that should learn how to spell, but *each* student! Thus it was necessary to put a word book into the students' hands. Sometimes the use of wordlists [*Wörterheft*] is recommended, but even this type of book does not satisfy our goal. In such a wordlist one leaves some pages empty for each initial letter and a student will occasionally enter important words in the available space in the same order in which those words occur during lessons. Such a wordlist could be helpful for some purposes, but it is an inadequate substitute for a word book if one wants to look up a word, for it either does not contain enough words or it takes an extremely long time to look up words, which becomes practically impossible. So a word *book* – but which one? One can only consider the two word books that have been published by the Schulbücher Verlag. Their large edition—which I want to call 'the large word book' for short—has various disadvantages with regards to my purposes. First, it is too expansive and therefore frequently too expensive for our rural population; second, because of its bulk it is difficult for the children to use; and third, it contains a significant number of words that a child never uses, especially many foreign words. On the other hand, it lacks many words that are necessary for the children to know. Partly those are words that have not been included perhaps because of their simplicity, e.g. *dann* [*then*], *wann* [*when*], *mir* [*me*, Dative], *dir* [you, Dative], in [*in, into*], etc. But it is exactly those easiest words that are frequently misspelled by children, and they are when the most unfortunate mistakes occur. On the other hand the large word book is missing many compounds and decompositions of compounds. But those words should be in a word book for elementary schools because children have great difficulty recognizing them as such. It often does not occur to them to look up the root word [*Stammwort*] of a compound (e.g. *Rauchfang* [*chimney*] – the children say *Raufang*). Or they recognize the word as a compound but they make an error when they decompose it: for the word *Einnahme* [revenue, receipts, proceeds] they look up *ein* [*a, one*] and *Name* [*name*], etc. This is why the large word book was not suitable for my purposes. But the short edition was totally useless too, because it lacked the most common and important words in everyday life. Indeed, this little volume is nearly a lexicon of just foreign words and thus precisely what I could not use. In this situation of need I made up my mind to dictate to my students (the fourth grade of a school with five grades) a word book. This word book contained around 2,500 key words. An even smaller word book would not have served its purpose. Those who have practical experience are able to understand the difficulties of this work, which should result in each student receiving a clean and correct copy of a word book, if at all possible, and in order to reach that goal the teacher must control almost every word each student has written. (It is not enough to spot check. I do not even want to begin talking about the demands on discipline.) When, after several months of work, the little word book was finished it proved itself to have been worthwhile: the improvement of spelling was astonishing. The orthographic conscience was awakened! But this process of writing a word book for oneself is usually not feasible, especially especially in a multi-grade classroom. But also also in schools with more grade-levels this procedure would be time-consuming and difficult, and those disadvantages are adequately outweighed by the advantages, which, doubtless, such a self-composed word book would have had over a ready-made purchased one. This is how I came to write the word book under consideration.

The problems that arose with the composition of the word book concern the selection and the order of the words. For the selection of words, the following principles were decisive for me:

(1) Only those words that students of Austrian elementary schools are familiar with should be included in the word book; regarding those words the listing should be complete. Thus, also many good German words which are not used in Austria, like *abgefeimt* [crafty, cunning], äffen [mock, ape], *bosseln* [emboss, mould], *erkleklich* [*erklecklich;* considerable], should be omitted. One has to use space sparingly since a big volume would make looking up words more difficult and make the book more expensive. Regarding words the student is familiar with, on the other hand, it is necessary that the word book be as complete

as possible for many reasons, not the least of which is: if the student often looks up words to no avail they will lose confidence, with the result being that they will no longer consult the word book.

(2) No word is too easy to be included, since I have experienced that *wo* [where] has been written with the "*h*" that indicates a long vowel, and *was* [what] with "*ss*".

(3) Compounds should be entered if they are either difficult for the child to recognize them as such, or if the looking up of the root words would easily lead to mistakes.

(4) Foreign words should only be entered if they are used universally. They ought to be translated into German if this is not too difficult and if the translation is not less understandable than the foreign word itself.

(5) Dialectical expressions should be entered only insofar as they have been admitted into the cultured language, like e.g. *Heferl* [*Häferl*; mug, little pot], *Packel* [small parcel], *Lacke* [puddle].

In some cases it is of course challenging to judge whether a word should be entered into the word book or not. Far more difficult, however, are the questions about how to arrange the words. Namely, in addition to the principle of alphabetic order, various clashing principles are decisive. Which principle becomes the determinative one in any given case quite often depends not infrequently on the subjective perception of the author. For instance, such a principle would be to affiliate the derivatives after the root word (that is, only the root word would be the keyword, with all the other derivatives following the keyword on the same line or on following lines. In the latter case the lines that follow are indented.) This principle clashes with that of alphabetic order. For instance, how should one arrange the words *alt* [old], *Altar* [altar], *Alter* [old age], *Altertum* [antiquity], *altertümlich* [antique]? Here we could have used alphabetic order, but this has the disadvantage that *alt* and *Alter*, which belong together, are separated by a word with a heterogeneous meaning. The grouping together of related words is already desirable for space-saving reasons. But this principle would demand that *Altertum* and *altertümlich* are also affiliated with *alt*, i.e. they should be moved before the word *Altar*. However, this arrangement would look unnatural, and finding complicated derivatives would become very difficult. I have arranged the words in the following way in this case:

alt, das Alter
der **Altar**
das **Altertum,** altertümlich
etc.

I mentioned this example here because it shows how the order of words is governed by various principles, the authority of which in relation to one another is difficult to justify. Perhaps some would recommend the principle of alphabetic order as the only governing principle. (For instance, this principle is carried out in Weide's word book.) But the purely alphabetic order, which pushes a heterogeneous word between closely related ones, then in my opinion demands too much of the child's ability to abstract. Due to the comprehension of words – and the important issue of saving space – purely alphabetic order often cannot be recommended. Likewise, any instance of clinging to a rigid principle leads to an arrangement that does not suit our purpose and must be abandoned – even if this would make the author's work far easier. Rather, it is necessary to compromise over and over. In one instance, the affiliation of a derivative after the root word readily leads to confusions; in another instance, this danger does not exist; in other instances one has to put the derivative in front of the root word; in some instances, one has to put a configuration of words besides the lexical entry, which explains the meaning of the lexical entry in order to prevent misunderstandings; in other cases, this is superfluous; etc., etc. It would be too much for me to justify my groupings for a larger number of cases. I have considered the accurate groupings of each case precisely and for a long time. Again and again psychological principles (where will the student look for a word, how does one guard against confusions in the best way possible) clash with grammatical ones (root word, derivative) and with the typographical use of space, with the well-organized look of the printed page, etc. The result is that a superficial judge will be met with seemingly arbitrary inconsequences everywhere, but those are caused by compromises between decisive principles.

Apart from emphasizing the keywords, I have used bold in all the cases where I wanted to make words or single letters especially apparent. It should not be difficult to understand the reason in each individual case. But it was also not advisable here to decide on the basis of one *single* principle whether or not a word should be printed in bold (e.g. to print all root words in bold, but not derivatives).

I have treated the letter "ß" as a simple *s*-sound for when the alphabetic order of words was the decisive factor. The usual arrangement where it follows "ss" seemed to me to be unnatural in a large number of cases. It also seemed likely to make the search for a word more difficult for children, e.g. when between *aus* [from, out] and *aussen* [*außen*; out, outside] the words *ausgiebig* [plentiful], *Auskunft* [information], *Ausnahme* [exception], etc. are inserted. The student reads *aus*, finds nothing under *ause*, and thinks, "Oh, then I already know how *ausen* is spelled." Admittedly, my arrangement produces some unnatural groupings since, according to present orthography "ß" is used for "*sz*" and for "ß", in those two cases "ß" would have a different place in the alphabet.

An additional word about putting the article in front of an key word: I think that this facilitates comprehension and prevents errors. I have added the article to all of the nouns (with the exception of some compounds) since the article indicates the noun as such. If one puts the article behind the noun it easily goes unnoticed by the child or the child relates it erroneously to the following word. The clarity of the column has not suffered from this new arrangement.

— Otterthal, April 22, 1925
The Author.
(Translated by Nickolas Calabrese and Désirée Weber)

die Amsel (blackbird)

KEY

adv.	adverb
bot.	botanical
gen.	genitive
intr.	intransitive
mil.	military
pl.	plural
rel.	related
so.	someone
sg.	singular
sth.	something
tech.	technical

A

das Aas, Aase oder Äser	carrion (sg. & pl.)
ab, ab und zu	off, on and off
die Abbildung	picture
das Abe	toilet
der Abend, heute abend, abends	evening, tonight, at night
das Abendmahl	Last Supper
das Abenteuer	adventure
aber	but
der Aberglaube, abergläubisch	superstition, superstitious
abermals	again
das Abführen	arresting, carrying away
der Abgeordnete	delegate
abgespannt = matt	worn-out = tired-out
der Abgrund, Abgründe	abyss, abysses
abhanden kommen	to go astray
der Abhang, Abhänge	slope, slopes
abhärten, die Abhärtung	to harden, hardening
der Ablaß, Ablässe	indulgence, indulgences
der Ableger	offshoot
ablösen, abgelöst	to replace, replaced
die Abnahme	inspection and approval
die Abneigung	dislike
das Abonnement, der Abonnent, abonnieren	subscription, subscriber, to subscribe
der Abort	toilet
der Abschied	taking leave
der Abschnitt	section/paragraph
abschüssig	precipitous
absehbare Zeit	foreseeable time
abseits	aside, off the beaten track
die Absicht, absichtlich	intention, intentional
absolut	absolute
abspenstig	alienating
abstammen, die Abstammung	descend, descent
der Abstand, Abstände	distance, distances
der Abstecher	detour
abstellen	to turn off
der Abstieg	descend
der Abszeß, Abszesse	abscess, abscesses
der Abt, Abte, Abtei	abbot, abbots, abbey
der Abteil, die Abteilung	compartment, department
abtun, abgetan	to dismiss, dismissed
abwärts	downhill
abwechseln, die Abwechslung	to alternate, alternation
abwesend, die Abweseheit	absent, absence
der Abzug, Abzüge	deduction, deductions/contact print, contact prints
abzweigen, die Abzweigung	to fork, fork
ach!	oh!, dear me!
die Achse, Radachse	axis, axle
die Achsel, Schulter	armpit, shoulder
acht (8), eine Acht, ein Achter, die achte Stunde, das Achte, achtzehn, achtzig	eight (8), an eight, eights, the eighth hour, the eighth, eighteen, eighty
achten, die Achtung, achtungsvoll	to respect, respect, respectful
achtgeben, gib acht!	to pay attention, pay attention!
achthaben	to watch, to take care
achtsam, die Achtsamkeit	attentive, attention
achtzehn, achtzig	eighteen, eighty
ächtzen	to groan
der Acker, Acker, ackern, der Ackerbau	farmland, arable land, to plough, farming
addieren, die Addition	to add, addition
der Adel, adelig	nobility, noble
die Ader	vein
adieu, Leb' wohl!	bye, take care!
der Adler	eagle
Adolf	Adolf
die Adresse, adressieren	address, to address
der Advent	advent (season)
der Advokat	lawyer
der Aeroplan	airplane
der Affe	monkey
affektiert	affected
Afrika, afrikanisch	Africa, African
der Agent, die Agentur	agent, agency
Agnes	Agnes
die Ahle	awl
ähneln	to resemble
ahnen, die Ahnung, ahnungslos	to suspect, suspicion, unsuspecting
ähnlich, die Ähnlichkeit	similar, similarity
der Ahorn	maple
die Ähre = Getreideähre	ear = ear of grain
der Akkord, Akkordarbeit	chord, piecework
der Akkumulator	accumulator

WORD BOOK

akkurat	accurate
der Akrobat	acrobat
der Akt	act
die Aktie, Aktienge-sellschaft	stock, stock corporation
der Alarm, alarmieren	alarm, to alarm
Albert, Albrecht	Albert, Albrecht
das Album	album
Alexander	Alexander
der Alkohol, alkoholisch	alcohol, alcoholic
alle, alles, vor allem	all, everything, above all
die Allee	tree-lined avenue
allein, alleinig	alone, sole
allenfalls	at best
aller...	all of/most (adv.)
allerdings	although
allerhand	a lot
Allerheiligen	All Saints Day
allerhöchst, allerletzt	highest of all, very last
allerlei	sundry
Allerseelen	All Souls Day
allgemein	common
allmächtig	almighty
allmählich	gradually
allwissend	all-knowing
die Alm	alpine pasture
das Almosen	alms
Alois, Aloista	Alois, Aloista
die Alpe	alp
die Alpen, der Älpler	Alps, alpine herdsman
das Alphabet, alphabetisch	alphabet, alphabetical
als	as
alsdann	then
also	thus
alt, älter, am ältesten, ältlich, das Alter, altern	old, older, oldest, elderly, age, to age
der Altar, Altare	altar, altars
alterieren	to alter
das Altertum, -tümer, altertümlich	antiquity, antiquities, ancient
altmodisch, altväterlich	old-fashioned, patriarchal
das Aluminium	aluminum
am = an dem	on the
am besten, am grössten usw.	best, highest, etc.
der Amboß, Ambosse	anvil, anvils
die Ameise	ant

amen!	amen!
Amerika, der Amerikaner, amerikanisch	America, the American, American
die Amme	wet nurse
die Ampel	lamp, sanctuary lamp
die Amsel	blackbird
das Amt, Ämter, amtieren	office, offices, to hold office
an, an dem = am; an das = ans at	at the; to the
der Anbau, anbauen	cultivation, to cultivate
anbieten	to offer
die Andacht, andächtig	devotion, devout
das Andenken	souvenir, memory
andere, anderer, anderes, ein andermal, ein anderes Mal, anders, and(e)-rerseits, anderseits	others, another time, differ-ent, on the other hand
ändern, die Änderung	to alter, alteration/to change, change
anders, anderswo	different, elsewhere
anderthalb	one and a half
der Andrang	throng, crowd
aneignen	to acquire
aneinander	adjoining
das Aneroidbarometer	aneroid barometer
der Anfall, Anfälle	fit, fits (illness)
der Anfang, Anfänge	beginning, beginnings
anfangen, anfangs	to begin, in the beginning
anfertigen, die Anfer-tigung	to manufacture, manu-facture
angeblich	alleged
der Angehörige	relative, kin
die Angel, angeln	hook, fishing rod, to fish
angenehm	pleasant
der Angriff	attack
die Angst, in Ängsten sein, angst und bang	fear, to be fearful, terribly frightened
ängstigen	to frighten, to be afraid
ängstlich, die Ängstlich-keit	fearful, fearfulness
anhänglich, die An-hänglichkeit	affectionate, affection
das Anhängsel	appendage
der Anis	anise
der Anker, ankern	anchor, to anchor
ankündigen, die Ankün-digung	to announce, announce-ment
die Ankunft	arrival
die Anlage	site, compound (of build-ings), layout
der Anlaß, Anlässe, anläßlich	occasion, occasions, on the occasion of

34

anmaßend, die Anmaßung	presumptuous, presumptuousness
die Anmerkung	annotation, remark
Anna	Anna
die Annehmlichkeit	amenity
Anno = im Jahr ...	in the year of
die Annonce = Anzeige	advert = announcement
annoncieren	to advertise
ans = an das	to the
ansässig	residing
anschaffen	to get, to buy
anschnauzen	to berate
die Ansicht	point of view
aussiedeln, die Aussied(e)-lung	to resettle, resettlement
anspannen	to tighten/to harness
der Anspruch, Ansprüche	claim, claims
die Anstalt	institution
der Anstand, Anstände	decency, manners
anständig	decent
anstatt	instead of
anstecken, die Ansteckung	to infect, infection
anstiften, der Anstifter	to instigate, instigator
ansträngen = anschirren	to harness = to hitch up
anstrengen (plagen), die Anstrengung	to strain (to enervate), strain
Anton, Antonia	Anton, Antonia
antun, angetan	to do sth. to so., to be taken by so.
die Antwort, antworten	response, to respond
anweisen, die Anweisung	to instruct, instruction
anwenden, die Anwendung	to apply, application
das Anwesen	estate
anwesend	to be present
der Anzug, Anzüge	suit, suits (clothing)
der Apfel, Äpfel	apple, apples
der Apostel, apostolisch	apostle, apostolic
der Apostroph	apostrophe
die Apotheke, der Apotheker	pharmacy, pharmacist
der Apparat	apparatus/device
der Appetit, appetitlich	appetite, appetizing
der Applaus, applaudieren	applause, to applaud
apportieren, apport!	to retrieve, retrieve!
der April	April
der Äquator	equator
das Ar: Flächenmass	acreage
arabische Ziffer	Arabic numeral
die Arbeit, arbeiten, der Arbeiter, Arbeiterin, -innen	work, to work, worker (male), worker (female), workers (female pl.)
arbeitslos, Arbeitslosigkeit	unemployed, unemployment
der Architekt	architect
arg, ärger, am ärgsten	bad, worse, worst
der Ärger, ärgerlich, ärgern	trouble, troublesome, to trouble
argwöhnisch	suspicious
der Arm, der Ärmel	arm, sleeve
arm, ärmer, am ärmsten, ärmlich, armselig	poor, poorer, poorest, needy, miserable
die Armut	poverty
arrangieren = einrichten	to arrange = to set up
der Arrest, arretieren	arrest, to arrest/to lock, to fix
die Art	kind/type/method
artig, die Artigkeit	polite, politeness
der Artikel	article
die Arznei	medicine
der Arzt, Ärzte, ärztlich	doctor, doctors, medical
die Asche, äschern	ashes/cinders, to strew with cinders
asten	to work hard
der Ast, Äste	branch, branches
die Astronomie, astronomisch	astronomy, astronomical
das Atelier	studio
der Atem, atemlos	breath, breathless
der Atlas, Atlasse oder Atlanten	atlas, atlases
atmen, die Atmung	to breath, breathing
die Atmosphäre, atmosphärisch	atmosphere, atmospheric
das Attentat	assassination
asen, die Asung = Futter	to forage, foraging = fodder
äsen, äsend	to graze, grazing
die Au, Auen	meadow, meadows
auch	also
der Auerhahn, -hähne	grouse (male, sg. & pl.)
die Auerhenne, -hennen	grouse (female, sg. & pl.)
auf, auf und davon, aufs = auf das	up/on/at, off and away, up/on/at the
aufbahren	to lay out
aufbewahren	to keep/to preserve
aufeinander	on top of each other
der Aufenthalt	stay/sojourn
die Auferstehung	Resurrection

das Atelier (studio)

auffallen, auffallend	to stand out, conspicuous
auffällig	conspicuous
die Aufführung	performance
die Aufgabe	assignment
aufgeregt	nervous/excited
aufhören	to finish/to stop
aufmerksam, die Aufmerksamkeit	attentive, attention
die Aufnahme	admission/recording/incorporation
aufpäppeln	to nurse back to health
aufpassen, aufgepasst	to pay attention, paid attention
aufrecht	upright
aufregen, aufgeregt, die Aufregung	to excite, excited, excitement
aufrichtig, die Aufrichtigkeit	honest, honesty
aufs = auf das	up/on/at the
der Aufsatz, Aufsätze	essay, essays
die Aufsicht	supervision
aufstapeln	to stack/to pile up
der Auftrag, -träge, auftragen	order, orders, to order
aufwärts	upward
der Aufzug, Aufzüge	elevator, elevators
das Auge, Augapfel, einäugig	eye, eyeball, one-eyed
der Augenblick	moment
die Augenbraue	eyebrow
das Augenlied	eyelid
der August (Monat)	August (month)
August, Augusta	August, Augusta
aus, aus und ein	from/out/of/off, off and on
die Ausdehnung	expansion
der Ausdruck, Ausdrücke	expression, expressions
ausdrücklich	explicit
auseinander	apart
außen, von außen	outside, from outside
außer, außerdem	except, besides
äußere, äußerste, äußerlich	outer, outermost, outward
außerhalb	outside of
äußern, die Äußerung	to state, statement
außerordentlich	exceptional/exceptionally
äußerst	extremely
ausführlich	extensive
die Ausführung	execution/carrying out
das Ausgeding	share of property for farmers on retirement
ausgezeichnet	excellent
ausgiebig	extensive/plentiful
ausgleichen, -geglichen	to balance, balanced
ausglitschen	to slip
aushalten	to endure/to sustain/to withstand
die Auskunft, Auskünfte	information (sg. & pl.)
das Ausland, Ausländer, ausländisch	abroad/foreign country, foreigner, foreign
ausleeren: ausgießen	to empty: to pour out
die Ausnahme	exception
ausnahmsweise	for a change/as an exception
ausrenken	to dislocate
ausrichten	to align
ausrotten	to exterminate
die Aussaat	sowing
der Ausschuß, Ausschüsse	committee, committees
die Aussicht	view
aussöhnen	to reconcile
ausstaffieren	to deck out
ausstatten, die Ausstattung	to fit out, outfit
ausstehen, ausgestanden	to endure, endured
die Ausstellung	exhibition
Australien	Australia
der Austritt	withdrawal/exit
auswärtig, auswärts	from outside, out of town/foreign, abroad
der Ausweis	identity document
auswendig	by heart
das Auto = Automobil	car = automobile
der Automat	automat
das Ave Maria	Hail Mary
das Aviso	advice
die Axt, Äxte	axe, axes

B

der Bach, Bäche	stream, streams
backen, backe oder bak, gebacken, du bäckst	to bake, bake, baked, you bake
der Bäcker, die Bäckerei	baker, bakery
Bad, Bäder, baden	bath, baths, to bathe
bähen	to toast
die Bahn, den Weg bahnen	path, to clear a path
der Bahnhof, -höfe, Bahnsteig	train station, train stations, platform
die Bahre, aufbahren	stretcher, to lay out

das Bajonett	bayonet
balancieren	to balance
bald, baldig	soon, early
der Balg, Bälge	rascal, rascals
balgen, die Balgerei	to horse round, horseplay
der Balken	beam
der Balkon	balcony
der Ball, Bälle	ball, balls
der Ballen, ballen, ballte, geballt	bale, to bale, baled, baled
der Ballon	balloon
der Balsam	balm
die Balz, balzen	courtship, to perform a mating dance
das Band (Streifen), Bänder	ribbon (band), ribbons
der Band (Buch), Bände	volume (book), volumes
die Bande	gang
bändigen, der Bändiger	to tame, tamer
der Bandit	bandit
bang, bänger, die Bängigkeit	anxious, more anxious, anxiety
die Bank (zum sitzen), Bänke, das Bänkchen	bench (to sit on), benches, little bench
die Bank (Geld-), Banken, die Banknote, der Bankier	bank (money), banks, bank note, banker
bar bezahlen, bares Geld (Aber: ein paar....)	to pay cash, cash
der Bär (Tier)	bear (animal)
die Baracke	barrack
Barbara	Barbara
barfuß, barfüßig	barefoot, barefoot
barmherzig, die Barmherzigkeit	merciful, mercy
der Barn = Krippe	manger = crib
barock, der Barockstil	Baroque, Baroque style
das Barometer	barometer
der Baron, die Baronin	baron, baroness
die Barriere	barrier
barsch	harsh
der Bart, Bärte, bärtig	beard, beards, bearded
der Baß, Bässe	bass, basses
der Basar	bazaar
der Bast	bast
basteln	to craft
die Batterie	battery
der Bau, Bauten, bauen	building, buildings, to build
der Bauch, Bäuche	stomach, stomachs

der Bauer, die Bäuerin, -innen, Bauernleute	farmer (male), farmers (female), farming people
der Baum, Bäume	tree, trees
baumeln	to dangle
bäumen, aufbäumen	to rear, to rear up
die Baumwolle	cotton
der Bausch, Bäusche, bauschen, bäuschig	wad, wads, to bulge, bulgy
bausen = durchzeichnen	to trace = to create a rubbing
der Beamte	civil servant
beben, das Erdbeben	to quake, earthquake
der Becher	cup
das Becken	basin
bedächtig	deliberate
bedeuten, die Bedeutung	to mean, meaning
bedienen, die Bedienung, der Bediente	to serve, server/service, servant
die Bedingung, unter der Bedingung	condition, under the condition
das Bedürfnis, -nisse	need, needs
die Beere, die Erdbeere	berry, strawberry
das Beet, Gartenbeet	bed, planting bed
der Befehl, befehlen, befahl, befohlen, du befiehlst, befiehlt	order, to order, ordered, ordered, you order, order
befriedigen	to satisfy
begegnen	to encounter
begehren	to desire
die Begierde, begierig	desire, eager/avid
der Begin, beginnen, began, begonnen	beginning, to begin, began, begun
begleiten (mitgehen), die Begleitung	to accompany (to go along), companion
das Begräbnis, -nisse	funeral, funerals
begreifen, -griff, -griffen	to understand, understood, understood
der Begriff	term, concept
behalten, -hielt, -hieltst	to keep, kept, kept/to retain
der Behälter	container
behilflich	helpful
die Behörde, behördlich	government agency, governmental
behutsam	gentle, careful
bei, beim = bei dem	at/by = at/by the (dative case)
die Beichte, beichten, der Beichtvater	confession, to confess, father confessor
beide, beides	both, both/either
beiderlei	on both counts
beiderseits	on both sides

beieinander	together
beiläufig	incidental
beileibe	by no means
beim = bei dem	at/by the (dative case)
das Bein	leg
beinahe	almost
das Beispiel, zum Beispiel	example, for example
beißen, biß, gebissen, du beißt, der Biß	to bite, bit, bitten, you bite, bite
die Beize, beizen	pickle, to pickle
beisetzen	to lay to rest
bejahen, bejahte, bejaht	to affirm, affirmed, affirmed
bekannt, der Bekannte, bekanntlich	familiar/famous, acquaintance, as is well known
die Bekleidung, Kleider	clothing, clothes
bekritteln	to cavil at
belehnen	to lend
beliebig	arbitrary
beliebt	popular
bellen	to bark
bemängeln	to criticize
das Benehmen, sich benehmen, benahm, benommen, benimmst, benimmt	behavior, to behave, behaved, behaved, you behave, behaves
der Bengel	rascal
benützen, benutzt	to use, used
das Benzin	gasoline
bequem, die Bequemlichkeit	comfortable, comfort
bereit, die Bereitschaft	ready, readiness
bereiten, die Bereitung	to prepare, preparation
bereits	already
der Berg, bergig	mountain, mountainous
bergab, bergauf	downhill, uphill
bergen : verborgen, barg, geborgen, du birgst, birgt	to hold, hidden, held, held, you hold, holds
Bernhard	Bernhard
der Bernhardiner	Saint Bernard dog
bersten, barst, geborsten	to burst, burst, burst
Berta	Bertha
berüchtigt	infamous
beschaffen	to obtain/to get hold of
beschäftigen	to employ/to keep occupied
bescheiden	modest
bescheren, die Bescherung	to give, giving of presents (at Christmas)
beschweren	to complain
beschwichtigen	to appease
der Besen, Besenstiel	broom, broomstick
der Besitz, besitzen, besass, besessen, du besitzt	possession, to possess, possessed, possessed, you possess
besondere, besonders	special, especially
besorgen, die Besorgung	to run an errand, errand
besser	better
bestätigen	to confirm
beste, zum besten halten, sein Bestes tun, bestens	best, to come off best, to do one's best, at best
das Besteck	silverware
die Bestie	beast
bestimmen, bestimmt	to determine, determined
der Besuch, besuchen	visit, to visit
betäuben, betäubt	to put under, put under
beten (Kirche), betete, gebetet	to pray (church), prayed, prayed
der Beton	concrete
betrachten	to regard
der Betrag, betragen, betrug, er beträgt	amount, to amount to…, amounted, amounts
betreiben, -trieb, -trieben, der Betrieb	to run, ran, run, operation (as in a business)
betrinken, -trank, betrunken	to get drunk, got drunk, drunk
betrüben, betrübt	to sadden, saddened
der Betrug, betrügen, -trogen	deception, to deceive, deceived
das Bett, betten = das Bett machen, zu Bette gehen	bed, to make the bed, to go to bed
betteln, der Bettler	to beg, beggar
beugen	to bend
die Beule	bump
die Beute	loot
der Beutel, beuteln	bag, to bag
bevor	before
bewaffnen	to arm
bewahren	to preserve
bewegen, die Bewegung	to move, movement
der Beweis, beweisen, bewiesen	proof, to prove, proven
bewirten, die Bewirtung	to cater, catering
bewundern, die Bewunderung	to admire, admiration
bewußtlos	unconscious
der Bezirk	district/county
der Bezirkshauptmann, die Bezirkshauptmannschaft	county commissioner, district administration
die Bibel	bible
die Bibliothek = Bücherei	library

WORD BOOK

biegen, bog, gebogen, biegsam, die Biegung	to bend, bent, bent, bendable, bend
die Biene	bee
das Bier	beer
bieten, bot, geboten	to bid, bid, bidden
das Bild, das Bildchen	picture, little picture
bilden	to picture, to educate
der Bildhauer	sculptor
die Bildung	education
billig, die Billigkeit	inexpensive, inexpensiveness
die Billion	trillion
bin, ich bin (von sein)	am, I am (from to be)
die Binde	bandage
binden, band, gebunden, das Band	to bind, bound, bound, band
der Binkel	jerk, dimwit
die Binse	rush (bot.)
die Birke	birch
die Birne	pear
die Birsch, birschen	stalking, to stalk
bis, bis dahin, bisher	until, until then, so far
der Biß (beißen), bissig	bite (to bite), biting
bißchen, ein bißchen	bit, a bit
der Bischof, Bischöfe	bishop, bishops
der Bissen	bite
bist, du bist	are, you are
die Bitte, bitten, bat, gebeten; bitte, gib mir...	request, to request, requested; please give me...
bitter	bitter
blamieren	to embarrass
blaß (bleich), blässer, die Blässe	pale (waxen), paler, paleness
die Blase	bladder
der Blasebalg, Blasebälge	bellows, bellows
blasen, blies, geblasen, du bläst	to blow, blew, blown, you blow
das Blatt (Pflanze), Blätter	leaf (plant), leaves
die Blatter = Blase	bladder
blau, bläulich	blue, bluish
das Blech	sheet metal/baking sheet
das Blei, bleiern = aus Blei	lead, leaden = of lead
bleiben, blieb, geblieben	to stay, stayed, stayed
bleich, bleichen	bleached, to bleach
der Bleistift	pencil
blenden	to blind
der Blick, blicken	look, to look
blind	blind
der Blitz, blitzen, Blitzableiter	lightning, to flash, lightning rod
das Bloch	log
der Block	block
blöd	dumb
blöken	to bleat
blond	blond
bloß	mere/bare
blühen, blühte, geblüht, die Blüte	to bloom, bloomed, bloomed, blossom
die Blume	flower
die Bluse	blouse
das Blut, bluten, blutig	blood, to bleed, bloody
die Blüte	blossom
der Bock, Böcke, bocken	buck, bucks, to buck
der Boden, Böden	floor, floors
der Bogen	bow
Böhmen, böhmisch	Bohemia, Bohemian
die Bohne	bean
bohren, der Bohrer	to drill, drill
der Böller	fire-cracker
der Bolzen	bolt
die Bombe	bomb
das Boot	boat
borgen	to salvage
die Borke, Borkenkäfer	bark, bark-beetle
die Börse	stock market
die Borste	bristle
bös, böse, bösartig	bad, wicked, malicious
boshaft, die Boshaftigkeit	vicious, viciousness
der Bote, die Botschaft	messenger, message
boxen, der Boxer	to box, boxer
brach	fallow
der Brand, Brände	fire, fires
der Branntwein	brandy
braten, briet, gebraten, du brätst, brät, der Braten	to roast, roasted, roasted, you roast, roasts, roast
brauchen	to need
brauen, der Brauer, die Bräuerei	to brew, brewer, brewery
braun, bräunlich	brown, brownish
die Brause	fizzy beverage
brausen	to roar/to fizz
die Braut, Bräute	bride, brides
der Bräutigam	groom
brav, die Bravheit	well-behaved, good behavior
bravo!	bravo!

brechen, brach, gebrochen, du brichst, bricht, brich!	to break, broke, broken, you break, breaks, break!
der Brei	mush
breit, die Breite	wide, width
die Bremse, bremsen	brake, to brake
brennen, brannte, gebrannt, der Brand	to burn, burned, burnt, fire
das Brett	board
die Brezel	pretzel
der Brief, Briefträger	letter, postman
das Brikett	briquette
die Brille	glasses, spectacles
bringen, brachte, gebracht	to bring, brought, brought
brödeln	to dawdle
der Brocken, einbrocken	chunk, to crumble/to get so. into trouble
brodeln	to simmer
die Brombeere	blackberry
die Bronze	bronze
die Brosche	brooch
das Brösel, bröseln	crumb, to crumble
das Brot, Brote, brotlos	bread, breads, unprofitable
der Bruch, Brüche	break, breaks
die Brücke	bridge
der Bruder, Brüder	brother, brothers
brühen, brühte, gebrüht	to blanch, blanched, blanched
brüllen	to bellow
brummen	to growl
der Brunnen	well
die Brust, Brüste	breast, breasts
die Brut, brüten, brütig	brood, to brood, broody
brutto: mit Verpackung	gross: with packaging
der Bub	boy
das Buch, Bücher	book, books
die Buche	beech
die Buchse	sleeve (tech.)
der Buchstabe, buchstabieren	letter, to spell
der Buckel, bucklig	hunchback, hunched
bücken	to bend down
die Bude	booth/hut/dump
die Budel	counter (in a store)
bügeln, das Bügeleisen	to iron, iron
die Bühne	stage
das Bukett	bouquet
der Bund, Bunde und Bünde	bond, bonds/alliance and alliances

das Bündel	bundle
der Bundesstaat	federal state
bunt	colorful
das Bureau = Kanzlei	office = court office
die Burg	castle
der Bürger, bürgerlich	citizen, civic
der Bürgermeister	mayor
der Bursch	boy
die Bürste, bürsten	brush, to brush
der Burzelbaum, -bäume	summersault, summersaults
burzeln	to tumble
der Busch, Büsche	bush, bushes
das Büschel	(small) bunch
die Buße, büßen	penance, to do penance
die Butte	vat
die Butter, Butterbrot	butter, buttered bread

C

Celsius (Thermometer)	centigrade (thermometer)
der Charakter	character
der Chauffeur (sprich: Schofför)	driver
die Chemie, chemisch	chemistry, chemical
China	China
der Chinese, chinesisch	Chinese man, Chinese
die Cholera = Brechruhr	cholera = diarrhea with vomiting
der Chor (Gesang)	choir (singing)
das Chor (Teil der Kirche)	choir (part of a church)
der Choral	chorale
der Christ, christlich, das Christentum, Christabend, Christtag, Christkind, usw.	Christ, Christian, Christianity, Christmas Eve, Christmas Day, baby Jesus, etc.
Christoph	Christopher
Christus	Jesus Christ
das Coupé (Abteil)	coupé (compartment)
der Coupon (Abschnitt)	coupon
der Cousin, die Cousine	cousin (male), cousin (female)

D

da	here/since
dabei	besides/near at hand/at the same time
das Dach	roof
der Dackel	dachshund
dadurch	that way

dafür	instead/after all/with regard to
daheim	at home
daher	therefore
dahier	here
damals	back then
die Dame	lady
damisch	ladylike
damit	thereby/so that
der Damm, Dämme	dam, dams
dämmern, die Dämmerung	to dawn, dawn
der Dampf, Dämpfe, dampfen	steam (sg. & pl.), to steam
der Dampfer = Dampfschiff	steamboat
danach	after/then/accordingly
daneben	alongside
der Dank, danken	thanks, to thank
dankbar, die Dankbarkeit	grateful, gratitude
dann	then/in that case
daran, darauf, daraus	at it/on it/to it/in it, after that/thereon, hence/out of it
darin, darinnen	in, within/inside (something)
der Darm, Därme	intestine, intestines
darüber	across it/about it/meanwhile/more
darum	therefore/around it/about it
darunter	among/underneath/under
das (Fürwort); in der Mundart: des, oder 's, 's Madel	the (pronoun); in dialect: the "the girl"
daß (Bindewort); in der Mundart: daß, "Schau, daß d' weiter kommst"	that (conjunction); in dialect: that, "See to it that ya scram."
dasselbe	the same
das Datum	date
dauern	to last
der Daumen	thumb
davon, davor	of it/off/thereof, beforehand
dazu	in addition
dazwischen	in between
der Dechant	dean
das Deck, Schiffdeck	deck, deck of a ship
die Decke, decken, gedeckt	cover/blanket, to cover, covered
der Deckel	lid
dehnen, dehnbar	to stretch, stretchable
die Deichsel	drawbar
dein, deine, deinige	your (sg. & pl.), yours
deinetwegen	on your account
das Dekagramm	decagram
die Dekoration, dekorieren	decoration, to decorate
delikat, die Delikatesse	delicate/delicious, delicacy
dem	to the (dative case)
demnächst	soon
der Demokrat, die Demokratie, demokratisch	democrat, democracy, democratic
demolieren	demolish
die Demonstration	demonstration
die Demut, demütig	humbleness, humble
dengeln (Sense)	to peen/sharpen (scythe)
denken, dachte, gedacht	to think, thought, thought
das Denkmal	monument
denn (Bindewort); in der Mundart: weil. Auch in Fragen: was denn, wo denn, wer denn usw.	for (conjunction); in dialect: because. Also in questions: what the…, where the…, who the…, etc.
das Depot	depot
der, des, den, dem	the (inflected), to the
derart, derartig	in such a way, such
derb, die Derbheit	crude/stout, crudeness/gruffness
dergleichen	such
derjenige	the one who (male)
dermassen	to such an extent
derselbe, desselben	the same, selfsame
des, dessen	whose (inflected)
deshalb	thus/therefore
die Desinfektion, desinfizieren	disinfection, to disinfect
desperat	desperate
dessen	whose
die Destillation, destillieren	distillation, to distill
desto, desto besser	the … the, so much the better
deswegen	therefore/that's why
deuten	to interpret
deutlich, die Deutlichkeit	clear, clarity
deutsch, der Deutsche, Deutschland, deutschnational	German, German (male), Germany, German national
der Dezember	December
dezi = ein Zehntel	deci = a tenth
die Dezimale, Dezimalwaage	decimal, decimal balance
der Dezimeter	decimeter

die Diagonale	diagonal
der Dialekt	dialect
der Diamant	diamond
die Diarrhöe = Durchfall	diarrhea = the runs
die Diät	diet
dich, in Briefen groß zu schreiben	you, capitalized in letters (accusative case)
dicht, die Dichte	dense, density
dichten, der Dichter	to write poetry, poet
dick, die Dicke	thick, thickness
das Dickicht	thicket
die, der, das	the (inflected)
der Dieb, diebisch	thief, thievish
der Diebstahl, Diebstähle	theft, thefts
diejenige	the one who (female)
die Diele	entrance hall
dienen, der Diener, die Dienerin, -innen	to serve, servant, maid servant, maid servants
der Dienst, der Dienstbote	service, servant
der Dienstag	Tuesday
dies, dies und das	this, this and that
dieselbe	the same
dieser, diese, dieses	this (inflected)
diesmal	this time
diesseits	on this side of
das Diktat, diktieren	dictation, to dictate
das Ding	thing
dingen, gedungen	to hire, hired
die Diphtherie, die Diphtheritis	diphtheria, diphtheritis
das Diplom	diploma
dir; in Briefen Dir	you (dative case); capitalized in letters
direkt	direct
die Direktion, Direktor	directorate, director
der Dirigent, dirigieren = leiten	conductor, to conduct (music)
die Dirne	young woman
diskutieren (sprechen)	to discuss (to speak)
disputieren (streiten)	to dispute (to argue)
die Distanz	distance
die Distel	thistle
die Disziplin	discipline
dividieren, die Division, der Dividend, der Divisor	to divide, division, dividend, divisor
der Diwan	divan
doch	yet/however
der Docht	wick
die Dogge	mastiff
der Doktor, Doktoren	doctor, doctors
das Dokument	document
der Dolch	dagger
der Dollar	dollar
der Dolmetsch	interpreter
der Dom	cathedral
das Domino	domino
die Donau	Danube
der Donner, donnern	thunder, to thunder
der Donnerstag	Thursday
doppeln, doppelt, der Doppler	to double, doubled, doubler
das Dorf, Dörfer, das Dörfchen	village, villages, hamlet
der Dorn, dornig	thorn, thorny
dörren	to dehydrate (as in vegetables)
dort, dorten, dorthin	there, there, thither
die Dose	tin
der Dotter, dottergelb	yolk, yolk-yellow
der Drache (Ungeheuer)	dragon (monster)
der Drachen (Papierdrachen)	kite (paper kite)
der Draht, drahten	wire, to wire
dran = daran	at it/of it
drängen, drängte, gedrängt	to push, pushed, pushed
drauf = darauf	on it/in it/to it/of it
draußen	outside
drechseln, der Drechsler	to turn, woodturner
der Dreck, dreckig	dirt, dirty
die Drehbank	lathe
drehen, drehte, gedreht, du drehst, dreht, die Drehung	to turn, turned, you turn, turns, turn/rotation
drei, die Drei = der Dreier, dreimal, dreißig, dreizehn	three, the three = the number three, three times, thirty, thirteen
das Dreieck, dreieckig	triangle, triangular
dreißig	thirty
dreiviertel, die Dreiviertelstunde	three quarters, three quarters of an hour
dreizehn	thirteen
dreschen, drosch, gedroschen, du drischst, er drischt, der Drescher	to thresh, threshed, threshed, you thresh, threshes, thresher
der Dreschflegel	flail
dressieren, die Dressur	to train, training (of animals)
drillen	to drill
drin, drinnen	inside (inflected)
dringen, drang, gedrungen	to urge, urged, urged

dringend	urgent
drinnen	inside, indoors
dritte, drittens	third, thirdly
das Drittel	a third
droben	up there
drohen, drohte, gedroht	to threaten, threatened, threatened
die Drohung	threat
die Drossel	thrush
drosseln (absperren)	to throttle (to block off)
drüben, drüber	over there, above/across
der Druck, drucken (Buch), drücken, der Drucker, die Druckerei	print, to print (book), to press, printer, print shop
drum, darum	therefore/around it
drunten, drunter	down there/underneath/among them, down
die Drüse	gland
du, in Briefen groß zu schreiben	you, capitalized in letters
ducken	to duck
dudeln	to tootle
der Duft, duften, duftig	smell, to smell (intr.), aromatic
dulden	to bear/to tolerate
dumm, dümmer, am dümmsten, die Dummheit	stupid, stupider, stupidest, stupidity
dumpf	dull
düngen, der Dünger	to fertilize, fertilizer
dunkel, die Dunkelheit	dark, darkness
dünn	thin
der Dunst	mist
durch, durchaus	through/across/by, entirely/by all means
durcheinander, ein Drucheinander	jumbled, jumble
der Durchmesser	diameter
durchs = durch das	through = through the
der Durschschnitt, durschnittlich	average, on average
durchsichtig	transparent
dürfen, durfte, darf, darfst	to be allowed to, was allowed to, allowed to, you are allowed to
dürftig	sparse
dürr, die Dürre	dry, drought
der Durst, dursten, durstig	thirst, to thirst, thirsty
die Dusche (Bad), abduschen	shower (bathroom), to shower
duster	dark/gloomy
das Duzend, duzendweise	dozen, by the dozen

das Dynamit	dynamite
die Dynamomaschine	dynamo

E

eben	even/just (adv.)
die Ebene, eben	plain, flat/level
ebenfalls	also/too
ebenso	just as/as well
das Echo	echo
echt, die Echtheit	authentic, authenticity
das Eck	corner
die Ecke, eckig, Eckzahn	corner, angular, eyetooth
edel	noble/refined
der Edelmut, edelmutig	gallantry, gallant
das Edelweiß	edelweiss (leontopodium)
Eduard	Edward
der Efeu	ivy
egal = gleichgültig	regardless, all the same = indifferent
die Egge = Ackergerät	harrow = agricultural implement
eggen, geeggt	to harrow, harrowed
die Ehe	marriage
ehe = bevor, ehemals	before = formerly
eher, ehestens	earlier/rather, at the earliest
die Ehre, ehren	honor, to honor
ehrerbietig	deferential
die Ehrfurcht, ehrfürchtig	reverence, reverential
der Ehrgeiz, ehrgeizig	ambition, ambitious
ehrlich, die Ehrlichkeit	honest, honesty
das Ei, die Eier	egg, eggs
die Eiche, eichen = aus Eichenholz	oak, oaken = made of oak wood
die Eichel	acorn
das Eichhörnchen, Eichkätzchen	squirrel, oak kitten
der Eid	oath
die Eidechse	lizard
der Eifer, eifrig	eagerness, eager
die Eifersucht, eifersüchtig	jealousy, jealous
eigen, die Eigenheit	of one's own/strange/idiosyncratic, singularity/strangeness/idiosyncrasy
eigenartig	peculiar
der Eigenname	proper name
der Eigennutz, eigennützig	self-interest, selfish
eigens	specifically

die Eigenschaft, Eigenschaftswort	characteristic, adjective
der Eigensinn, eigensinnig	obstinacy, obstinate
eigentlich	actually/essentially
das Eigentum, -tümer	possession, owner
eigentümlich	peculiar
eignen, sich eignen	to be suitable, to be suited
die Eile, eilen, eilig, eilends	hurry, to hurry, in a hurry, instantly
das Eilgut, Eilgüter	express freight, express goods
der Eimer	bucket
ein, einer, eine, eines	a (an), one, (inflected), of a (an)
einander	each other
einbilden, die Einbildung	to imagine, imagination
einbrechen, der Einbrecher	to burgle, burglar
der Einbruch, Einbrüche	burglary, burglaries
der Eindruck, Eindrücke	impression, impressions
einer, eine, eines	a (an), (inflected), a (an)/ one, one (inflected)
der Einer	unit/the number one
einerlei	all the same
einerseits	on the one hand
einfach, die Einfachheit	simple, simplicity
der Eingang, Eingänge	entry, entries
die Eingeweide	innards
einheimisch	native/local
einheizen	to heat/to light a fire
einholen	to catch up/to obtain/ to seek
einig	united
einige, einiges, einigemal	a few, something/a thing or two, a few times
einkehren	to stop in (for a bite)
das Einkommen	income
einladen, die Einladung	to invite, invitation
einmal, einmalig	once, unique
das Einmaleins	multiplication table
einmengen	to mix
die Einöde	wilderness, solitude
einpferchen	to corral
einpökeln	to cure (meat)
einpuppen	to cocoon
einquartieren, die Einquartierung	to quarter, quarters
einrücken	to move in/to enlist/to indent
eins, die Eins = der Einser	one, the one = the number one
einsam, die Einsamkeit	lonely, loneliness
die Einschicht, einschichtig	single layer, single-layered
einschränken	to restrict
einsegnen, die Einsegnung	to consecrate, consecration
einseitig, die Einseitigkeit	one-sided, one-sidedness
der Einsiedler, die Einsiedlerei	hermit, hermitage
einspannen	to harness (a horse)
einsperren	to lock so. up
einst, einstmals	once, in times past
einstecken	to pocket
einstöckig	one-storied
einstweilen	temporarily
einträglich	lucrative
der Eintritt	entry/admittance
einwärts	inward
der Einwohner	inhabitant
einzeln, die Einzelheit	particular/single, particular/ detail
einzig	singly
das Eis, eisig, eiskalt	ice, icy, ice cold
das Eisen, eisern	iron, ironclad
die Eisenbahn	railroad
eitel, die Eitelkeit	vain, vanity
der Eiter, eitern, eit(e)rig	pus, to fester, purulent
das Eiweiß	egg white
der Ekel, ekeln, ekelhaft	disgust, to be disgusted, disgusting
elastisch, die Elastizität	elastic, elasticity
der Elefant	elephant
elegant	elegant
elektrisch, elektrisieren, die Elektrizität	electric, to electrify, electricity
die Elektrotechnik, der Elektrotechniker	electrical engineering, electric engineer
das Element	element
elend, das Elend	miserable, misery
elf, die Elf = der Elfer, elfte	eleven, eleven = the number eleven, eleventh
Elisabeth, Elise	Elizabeth, Elise
Ella	Ella
der Ellbogen	elbow
die Elle	ell/yardstick, ulna
die Elipse, eliptisch	ellipsis, elliptical
Elsa	Elsa
die Eltern	parents

WORD BOOK

das Email, das Emailgeschirr, emaillieren	enamel, enamelware, to enamel
Emil	Emil
Emma, Emmerich	Emma, Emmerich
der Empfang, empfangen, der Empfänger	reception, to receive, receiver
empfehlen, empfahl, empfohlen, du empfiehlst, empfiehlt, die Empfehlung	to recommend, recommended, recommended, you recommend, recommends, recommendation
empfinden, empfand, empfunden, die Empfindung	to sense, sensed, sensed, sense/to feel, felt, felt, feeling
empfindlich	sensitive
empor	aloft
empören, empörend, die Empörung	to outrage so., outrageous, outrage
emsig	industrious/busy
das Ende, zu Ende, enden, endigen	end, over, to end, to end
endlich	finally
endlos	infinite
die Energie, energisch	energy, energetic/vigorous
eng, die Enge	tight /narrow, tightness / narrowness
der Engel	angel
England, der Engländer, englisch	England, Englishman, English
der Enkel, die Enkelin, -innen	grandson, granddaughter, granddaughters
enorm	enormous
entbehren, die Entbehrung	to miss/to do without, deprivation
entblößen	to expose/to uncover
entdecken, der Entdecker, die Entdeckung	to explore, explorer, exploration
die Ente, der Enterich	duck, drake
entfernen, die Entfernung	to distance, distance
entgegen	contrary to/against
der Entgelt, entgelten	remuneration, to remunerate
entgleisen, die Entgleisung	to derail, derailment
entlang	along
entlassen, die Entlassung	to lay off, layoff
entlegen	remote
entrüsten, die Entrüstung	to fill with indignation/to outrage so., indignation/ outrage
entschieden	decided
entschließen, -schlossen	to decide, decided
der Entschluß	decision
entschuldigen, die Entschuldigung	to excuse, excuse
entsetzen, entsetzt	to appall, appalled
entsetzlich	appalling
entstehen, -stand, -standen, die Entstehung	to emerge, emerged, emerged, emergence/ to originate, originated, originated, origination
entstellen, entstellt	to deform, deformed
enttäuschen, die Enttäuschung	to disappoint, disappointment
entweder	either
entwickeln, die Entwick(e)-lung	to develop, development
entzücken, entzückend	to delight, delightful
entzünden, die Entzündung	to inflame, inflammation
entzwei	in pieces/in two
der Enzian	gentian
er	he
erbarmen, erbärmlich	to move so./to take pity on, pitiful
der Erbe, erben	heir (male), to inherit
erblicken	to see, to espy
erbrechen, -brach, -brochen	to vomit, vomited, vomited
die Erbse	pea
der Erdapfel, Erdäpfel	potato, potatoes
die Erde, Erdachse	earth, axis of the Earth
das Erdbeben	earthquake
die Erdbeere	strawberry
ereignen, das Ereignis, -nisse	to occur, occurrence, occurrences
erfahren, die Erfahrung	to experience, experience
erfinden, -fand, -funden, der Erfinder, die Erfindung	to invent, invented, invented, inventor, invention
der Erfolg	success
ergänzen, die Ergänzung	to add, addition/to complement, complement
erhalten, -hielt, -halten	to preserve, preserved, preserved
erhitzen, -hitzte, -hitzt	to heat up, heated up, heated up
erholen, die Erholung	to recover, recuperation
erinnern, die Erinnerung	to remember, memory
erkennen, -kannte, -kannt	to recognize, recognized, recognized
erklären, die Erklärung	to explain, explanation
der Erlagschein	payment slip
erlauben, die Erlaubnis	to permit, permission
erleben, das Erlebnis, -nisse	to experience, experience, experiences
die Erle	alder
erlöschen, -losch, -loschen, erlischt	to expire, expired, expired, expires

46

WITTGENSTEIN

erlösen, die Erlösung	to redeem, redemption
ermahnen, die Ermahnung	to reprimand, reprimand/to admonish, admonition
der Ernst, ernst, ernstlich	gravity, grave, gravely
Ernst (Name)	Ernest (name)
die Ernte, ernten	harvest, to harvest
erobern, die Eroberung	to conquer, conquest
erquicken	to refresh
erraten	to guess
erreichen	to reach/to achieve
der Ersatz, ersetzen	substitution, to substitute
erscheinen, -schien, -schienen	to appear, appeared, appeared
erschrecken (vor etwas), erschrak, erschrocken, du erschrickst, er erschrickt; jemanden erschrecken, erschreckte, erschreckt, du erschreckst mich	to be frightened (at, by), frightened, frightened, you are frightened, he is frightened; to frighten so., frightened, frightened, you frighten me
ersetzen, -setzte, -setzt	to replace, replaced, replaced
erst	only just/not until
erste, erstens	first, first of all
ersticken	to suffocate
erträglich	tolerable
das Erträgnis, -nisse	income/revenue (sg. & pl.)
ertränken, -tränkte, -tränkt	to drown, drowned, drowned
ertrinken, -trank, -trunken	to drown, drowned, drowned
erwähnen	to mention
erwarten, die Erwartung	to expect, expectation
erwerben, -warb, -worben	to acquire, acquired, acquired
erwidern	to reply
erwischen	to catch (red-handed)
das Erz	ore
erzählen, die Erzählung	to tell, tale
erzeugen, die Erzeugung	to create, creation/to produce, production
erziehen, -zog, -zogen, die Erziehung	to raise, raised, raised, upbringing/to educate, educated, educated, education
es, es ist gut	it, it is good
der Esel	donkey
die Esse = Feuerherd	hearth = fireplace
das Essen, essen, aß, gegessen, du ißt, iß!, eßbar	food, to eat, ate, eaten, you eat, eat!, edible
die Essenz	essence
der Essig	vinegar

die Etagere = Stelle	shelves = wall rack
etliche, etliche Male	a number of, a number of times
etwas	some
euch, in Briefen groß zu schreiben	you (pl.), capitalized in letters
euer, eure, eures, eurem, euren, euretwegen, eurige	your (inflected), yours (inflected), because of you, your (pl.)
die Eule	owl
Europa, der Europäer, europäisch	Europe, the European, European
das Euter	udder
Eva	Eva
evangelisch, das Evangelium	Protestant, Gospel (New Testament)
eventuell	possibly
ewig, die Ewigkeit	eternal, eternity
das Exemplar	exemplar/sample
exerzieren	to exercise/to drill
existieren, die Existenz	to exist, existence
expedieren	to dispatch
die Expedition : Beförderung	dispatch : shipping
das Experiment = Versuch	experiment = trial
explizieren	to explicate/to interpret
explodieren, die Explosion	to explode, explosion
expreß, der Expreßbrief	express, express letter
extra	extra

F

die Fabel, fabelhaft	fable, fabulous
die Fabrik, der Fabrikant, die Fabrikation	factory, manufacturer, manufacture
fabrizieren	to manufacture
das Fach, Fächer	subject, subjects/compartment, compartments
fächeln, der Fächer	to fan, fan
fachen, anfachen	to kindle sth., to fan
die Fackel, Fackelzug	torch, torch parade
fädeln, einfädeln	to thread, to thread/to set about
der Faden, Fäden	thread, threads
fähig, die Fähigkeit	capable/competent, skill/competence
die Fahne	flag
fahren, fuhr, gefahren, du fährst, er fährt, die Fuhr	to drive, drove, driven, you drive, he drives, cartload
der Fahrplan, Fahrpläne	timetable, timetables
das Fahrrad, Fahrräder	bicycle, bicycles
die Fahrt	drive/trip in a vehicle

WORD BOOK

faktisch	factual
der Faktor	factor
der Falke	falcon
der Fall, Fälle	case, cases (as in case study)
die Falle (Mausefalle)	trap (mouse trap)
fallen, fiel, gefallen, du fällst, fällt	to fall, fell, fallen, you fall, falls
fällen = umschlagen; fälle, gefällt	to fell = to cut down; fells, felled
fällig	due
falls	in case
der Falott	crook
falsch, die Falschheit	false, falsity
fälschen	to forge
die Falte, falten, faltig	fold, to fold, folded/wrinkled
der Falter	butterfly
der Falz, falzen	sharp crease in book pages, to fold/to crease
die Familie, familiär	family, familiar
der Fang, Fänge	catch (sg. & pl.)
fangen, fing, gefangen, du fängst, fängt	to catch, caught, caught, you catch, catches
die Farbe, färben, farbig	color, to color, colored
die Farm, der Farmer	farm, farmer
das Farnkraut	bracken
das Faß, Fässer	barrel, barrels
der Fasching	carnival
faseln	to drivel
die Faser, faserig	fiber, fibrous
fassen, faßte, gefaßt, du faßt	to hold, held, held, you hold/to comprehend, comprehended, comprehended, you comprehend
die Fassung	composure/draft (of a text)/lamp socket
fast = beinahe	almost = nearly
das Fasten, fasten, Fasttag	fasting, to fast, fast day
fauchen	to hiss
faul = träg, die Faulheit	lazy = lethargic, laziness
faul = verfault, die Fäulnis	decayed = rotten, rot
faulenzen, der Faulenzer	to be lazy, lazybones
die Faust, Fäuste	fist, fists
der Fäustling	mitten
der Fauteuil = Lehnstuhl	fauteuil = armchair
die Faxe, Faxen machen	grimace, to grimace
der Februar, der Feber	February, February
fechsen, die Fechsung	to harvest, harvest
fechten, focht, gefochten, du fichst, er ficht, der Fechter	to fence, fenced, fenced, you fence, he fences, fencer
die Feder	feather
die Fee	fairy
fegen, der Feger	to sweep, sweep
fehlen	to lack, to miss
der Fehler	mistake
die Feier, feiern, Feierabend; Feiertag	celebration, to celebrate, time off; holiday
feig, die Feigheit, der Feigling	cowardly, cowardice, coward
die Feile, feilen	file, to file
fein, die Feinheit	fine, fineness
der Feind, die Feindin, -innen, feindlich, die Feindschaft	enemy, enemy (female), enemies (female), hostile, enmity
das Feld	field
der Feldherr	general/commander
der Feldspat	feldspar
die Felge	rim
Felix	Felix
das Fell	fur
der Fels, der Felsen, felsig	rock, boulder, rocky
das Fenster	window
Ferdinand	Ferdinand
der Ferialtag	vacation day
die Ferien	vacation
das Ferkel	piglet
fern, die Ferne, ferner	far, distance (as in faraway), further
die Ferse	heel
fertig, verfertigen	finished, to manufacture
die Fertigkeit	skill
fesch	fetching
fesseln, die Fessel	to tie up, bond/shackle
fest, die Festigkeit	firm, firmness
das Fest, Festtag	feast, holiday
die Festung	fortress
das Fett, fett, einfetten	fat, fat, to grease
der Fetzen, fetzen	shred, to shred
feucht, die Feuchtigkeit	moist, moisture
das Feuer, feurig, Feuersbrunst, Feuerwehr	fire, fiery, blaze, firefighters
der Fiaker	fiacre, horse-drawn carriage
die Fibel	first reader/primer
die Fichte	spruce
fidel = lustig	gay = merry
das Fieber, fiebern	fever, to have a fever
die Fiedel = Geige; fiedeln	fiddle = violin; to fiddle
die Figur	figure

das Eichhörnchen, Eichkätzchen (squirrel, oak kitten)

die Filiale	branch (of a business)
der Film, filmen	film, to film
der Filter, filtrieren	filter, to filter
der Filz, filzig	felt, felted
die Finanz, Finanzwache	finance, customs
finden, fand, gefunden, der Finder	to find, found, found, finder
findig	resourceful/ingenious
der Finger	finger
der Fink	finch
finster, die Finsternis, -nisse	dark, darkness/gloomy, gloom (sg. & pl.)
die Firma, Firmen, das Firmenschild	company, companies, company nameplate
firmen, die Firmung	to confirm so., Confirmation
der Firn	firn
der Firnis, des Firnisses, firnissen	varnish, varnish (genitive), to varnish
der First = Dachfirst	ridge = roof ridge
der Fisch, fischen, der Fischer	fish, to fish, fisherman
die Fisole	string bean
fix, fix und fertig	quick (in the sense of nimble), exhausted
fixieren	to fixate (on)
der Fixstern	fixed star
flach, die Fläche	flat, flat surface/area
der Flachs	flax
flackern	to flicker
der Fladen	pancake/flat cake
die Flagge, beflaggen	flag, to flag
die Flamme, flammen	flame, to flame
der Flanell	flannel
die Flasche	bottle
flattern	to flap
flau	weak
der Flaum, flaumig, Flaumfeder	fluff, fluffy, down feather
die Flechse : Sehne	sinews : tendon
die Flechte	lichen
flechten, flocht, geflochten, du flichst, flicht	to braid, braided, braided, you braid, braids
der Fleck, fleckig	stain, stained
der Flecken, Marktflecken	spot, market town
die Fledermaus, -mäuse	bat, bats
der Flegel, die Flegelei, flegelhaft	boor, boorishness, boorish
fliehen	to flee
der Fleiß, fleißig	diligence, diligent
das Fleisch, fleischig	meat, meaty
der Fleischer = Fleischbauer	butcher
flennen	to cry/to weep
fletschen	to bare teeth, to snarl (as of a dog)
flicken, die Flickerei	to patch, patchwork
der Flieder	lilac
die Fliege	fly
fliegen, flog, geflogen, der Flieger	to fly, flew, flown, flier
fliehen, floh, geflohen, du fliehst, flieht	to flee, fled, fled, you flee, flees
fließen, floß, geflossen	to flow, flowed, flowed
das Fließpapier	blotting paper
flimmern	to flicker
flink	swift/nimble
die Flinte	shotgun
die Flocke, flockig	flake, flaky
der Floh, Flöhe	flea, fleas
Florian	Florian
das Floß, Flöße, flößen	raft, rafts, to raft
die Flosse = Fischflosse	fin = fin of a fish
die Flöte, flöten	flute, to play the flute
flott	quick
der Fluch, Flüche, fluchen	curse, curses, to curse
die Flucht, flüchten	escape, to escape
flüchtig, die Flüchtigkeit	fleeting, fleetingness/carelessness
der Flug, Flüge, Flugzeug	flight, flights, airplane
der Flügel	wing
flügge	fledged
flugs	at once/in a jiffy
die Flur	meadow
der Fluß, des Flusses, Flüsse	river, of the river (genitive), rivers
flüssig, die Flüssigkeit	liquid, liquid
flüstern	to whisper
die Flut, Fluten	flood, to flood
das Fohlen	foal
die Föhre	pine
die Folge, folgen	succession, to succeed/consequence, to follow
folgendermaßen	as follows
folgsam, die Folgsamkeit	obedient, obedience
die Folter, foltern	torture, to torture
foppen	to tease
fordern = verlangen	to demand = to require

fördern, befördern	to promote/to support, to advance so.
die Forelle	trout
die Form, formen	form, to form
die Formel	formula
förmlich	formal/official
forschen, der Forscher	to research, researcher
der Forst, forsten	forest, to care for the forest
der Förster	forester
fort, sofort	gone, at once
fortpflanzen	to reproduce
der Fortschritt	progress
fortsetzen, die Fortsetzung	to continue, continuation
fortwährend	continuous
die Fracht, Frachtbrief	freight, consignment note
der Frack, Fräcke	tailcoat, tailcoats
die Frage, fragen, fragte	question, to ask, asked
die Fraisen	cramps
der Frank : Münze	franc : coin
frankieren	to stamp (a letter)
Frankreich	France
die Franse, fransen	fringe, to fringe
Franz, Franziska	Franz, Frances/Francine
der Franzose, französisch	Frenchman, French
der Fratz	brat
der Fraß	muck (of food)
die Frau, das Fräulein	woman, young lady
frech, die Frechheit	sassy, sassiness
frei, die Freiheit, im Freien	free, freedom, outdoors
freigebig, die Freigebigkeit	generous, generosity
das Freihandzeichnen	freehand drawing
freilich	indeed/certainly
der Freitag	Friday
freiwillig	voluntary
fremd, die Fremde	foreign, foreign countries
das Fremdwort, -wörter	foreign word, words
das Fressen, fressen, fraß, gefressen, du frißt, friß!, der Fraß	animal food, to eat, ate, eaten, you eat, eat! (of an animal), grub
fretten, das Gefrett	to hassle, hassle
die Freude, freudig	joy, joyful/delight, delighted
freuen	to be glad/to be delighted
der Freund, die Freundin, -innen, die Freundschaft	friend, friend (female), friends (female), friendship
freundlich	friendly
der Frevel, freveln	outrage/sacrilege, to commit an outrage/a sacrilege
der Friede, friedlich	peace, peaceful
der Friedhof, Friedhöfe	graveyard, graveyards
Friedrich	Friedrick
frieren, fror, gefroren	to freeze, froze, frozen
frisch	fresh
der Friseur = Haarschneider	hairdresser
frisieren, die Frisur	to do so.'s hair, haircut
die Frist	deadline
Fritz	Fritz
froh	glad
fröhlich, die Fröhlichkeit	cheerful, cheerfulness
fromm, die Frömmigkeit	pious, piety
der Fronleichnam	Corpus Christi
die Front	front
der Frosch, Frösche	frog, frogs
der Frost, frostig, frösteln	frost, frosty, to shiver
frotzeln, die Frotzelei	to tease, teasing
die Frucht, Früchte	fruit, fruits
fruchtbar, die Fruchtbarkeit	fertile, fertility
früh, früher, frühestens, die Frühe, in der Früh	early, earlier, earliest, morning, in the early morning
das Frühjahr	spring
der Frühling	spring
das Frühstück, frühstücken	breakfast, to have breakfast
frühzeitig	early on/premature
der Fuchs, Füchse	fox, foxes
fuchteln	to brandish
fuchtig	livid
das Fuder : ein Fuder Holz	cartload : cartload of wood
die Fuge	joint
fügen	to joint
fühlen, das Gefühl	to feel, feeling
der Fühler	feeler
die Fuhre, das Fuhrwerk	load, wagon
führen, der Führer	to lead, leader/to guide, guide/to command, commander
die Fülle : Füllung	plenty : filling
füllen : vollfüllen	to fill : to fill up
das Füllen : Pferd	foal : horse
der Fund	find/discovery
das Fundament	foundation
fünf, die Fünf = der Fünfer; fünfmal, fünfte	five, the five = the number five; five times, fifth
fünfzehn, fünfzig	fifteen, fifty
der Funke, funkeln	spark, to sparkle

WORD BOOK

funktionieren	to function
für, fürs = für das	for, for the (abbrev.) = for the
die Furche	furrow
die Furcht, fürchten, furchtbar, fürchterlich, furchtsam	fear, to fear, awful, fearsome, fearful
das Furnier	veneer
die Fürsorge	care
der Fürst, fürstlich	prince, princely
die Furt	ford
der Furunkel	furuncle/boil
das Fürwort	pronoun
der Fuß, Füße, Fußboden, Fußgänger usw.	foot, feet, floor, pedestrian, etc.
der Fusel : Schnaps	hooch : schnapps
das Futter, füttern	fodder, to feed
das Futteral	case (e.g. for spectacles)

G

die Gabe	gift
die Gabel, gabeln	fork, to fork
gackern	to cackle
gähnen	to yawn
die Gala	gala
die Galerie	gallery
der Galgen	gallows
die Galle	gall/gallbladder
der Galopp, galoppieren	gallop, to gallop
die Galosche	galosh
die Gamasche	gaiter
der Gang, Gänge	corridor, corridors
gängeln	to boss so. around
die Gans, Gänse, der Gänserich	goose, geese, gander
ganz, gänzlich	whole, complete/entire, entirely
gar, gar nicht	even (adv.), not at all
die Garage	garage
die Garantie, garantieren	guaranty, to guarantee
der Garaus, den Garaus machen	horror, to do so. in (ironic)
die Garbe	sheaf
die Garderobe	wardrobe
gären, gärte, gegoren oder gegärt, die Gärung	to ferment, fermented, fermented, fermentation
das Garn	yarn
garnieren	to garnish
die Garnitur	set/suite

garstig	nasty
der Garten, Gärten	garden, gardens
der Gärtner	gardener
das Gas, gasförmig	gas, gaseous
der Gasometer	gasometer
die Gasse, das Gäßchen	alley, alleyway
der Gast, Gäste	guest, guests
das Gasthaus	tavern/inn
das Gastmahl	banquet
der Gastwirt	innkeeper
der Gatte : Mann; Gattin	spouse : husband; wife
die Gattie = Unterhose	undies = underpants
die Gattung	species
der Gaul, Gäule	hack, hacks (as in horse)
der Gaumen	palate
der Gauner, die Gaunerei	trickster, trickery
das Gebäck : Bäckerei	pastry : bakery
gebären, gebar, geboren, sie gebiert	to bear, bore, born, she bears
das Gebäude	building
geben, gab, gegeben, du gibst, gibt, gib her!	to give, gave, given, you give, gives, give it!
das Gebet	prayer
das Gebiet	area
das Gebirge, gebirgig	mountains, mountainous
das Gebiß, Gebisse	denture, dentures
das Gebot	command
der Gebrauch, gebrauchen	use/practice, to use
die Gebühr, gebühren	charge/fee, to be due to so.
die Geburt, Geburtstag	birth, birthday
das Gebüsch	shrubbery
das Gedächtnis, -nisse	memory, memories
der Gedanke, gedankenlos	thought, thoughtless
das Gedärm	intestines
gedeihen, gedieh, gediehen	to flourish, flourished, flourished
das Gedicht	poem
gediegen	refined
das Gedränge	jostle/crowding
die Geduld, geduldig	patience, patient
die Gefahr, gefährlich	danger, dangerous
das Gefälle	slope
gefallen, gefiel, du gefällst, einen Gefallen tun	to please, pleased, you pleased so., to do so. a favor
gefällig, die Gefälligkeit	pleasant/accommodating, favor
das Gefängnis, -nisse	prison, prisons
das Gefäß	vessel

das Gefieder	plumage
das Geflügel	poultry
gefräßig	voracious
das Gefrett	hassle
gefrieren, gefroren, das Gefrorene	to freeze, frozen, ice cream
das Gefühl	feeling
gegen	against
die Gegend	region
gegeneinander	against each other
gegenseitig	mutual
der Gegenstand, Gegenstände	item/object, items/objects
das Gegenteil, im Gegenteil	contrary/opposite, on the contrary
gegenüber	vis-à-vis
die Gegenwart, gegenwärtig	present, present/at present
der Gegner	opponent
der Gehalt, Gehalte	salary, salaries
das Gehäuse	housing/casing (as of a clock)
geheim, das Geheimnis, -nisse	secret, secret, secrets
gehen oder gehn, ging, gegangen, ich gehe, gehst, geht, geh!	to go, went, gone, I go, you go, goes, go!
der Gehilfe	assistant
das Gehirn	brain
das Gehör	hearing
gehorchen, der Gehorsam	to obey, obedience
gehörig	obedient
der Geier	vulture
die Geige, geigen	violin, to play the violin
die Geiß, Geißen	goat, goats
die Geißel = Peitsche	flagellum = whip
der Geist, geistig	spirit/mind, spiritual/mental
geistlich, der Geistliche	clerical, cleric
der Geiz, geizig, Geizhals	stinginess, stingy, cheapskate
das Gelächter	laughter
das Geländer	banister
gelb, gelblich	yellow, yellowish
das Geld	money
gelehrig	teachable/apt/intelligent
gelehrt, der Gelehrte	scholarly, scholar
das Geleise	track (as of a train)
das Gelenk, gelenkig	joint, flexible
gelingen, gelang, gelungen	to succeed, succeeded, succeeded
die Gelse	gnat
gelten, galt, gegolten, es gilt	to count, counted, counted, it counts
gemächlich	leisurely
der Gemahl, die Gemahlin, -innen	husband, wife, wives
das Gemälde	painting
gemein, die Gemeinheit	mean, meanness
die Gemeinde, Gemeinderat	community/municipality, community council/municipal council
gemeinsam	together
das Gemenge	melee
die Gemse, Gemsbock	chamois, chamois buck
das Gemüse	vegetable
gemütlich, die Gemütlichkeit	cozy, coziness
genau, die Genauigkeit	precise, precision
der Gendarm : Schutzmann	gendarme : country constable
der General	general (military)
das Genick	neck
genieren = schämen (sprich: schenieren)	to feel embarrassed, to be embarrassed = to be ashamed
genießen, genoß, genossen	to enjoy, enjoyed, enjoyed
genug	enough
genügen, genügend	to suffice, sufficient
der Genuß, Genüsse	pleasure, pleasures
die Geographie, geographisch	geography, geographical
die Geometrie, geometrisch	geometry, geometrical
Georg	George
das Gepäck : Reisegepäck	luggage : travel luggage
gerade	just/straight
geraten, geriet, es gerät, aufs Geratewohl	to get into sth., got into sth., gets into sth., on the off-chance
geräumig	spacious
das Geräusch	sound
gerben, der Gerber	to tan, tanner
gerecht, die Gerechtigkeit	just/fair, justice/fairness
das Gericht	court
gering, nicht im geringsten	slight, not in the slightest
gerinnen, geronnen	to clot, clotted
das Gerippe	carcass
der Germ = Hefe	yeast
der Germane, germanisch	German (person), German
gern, gerne	glad, gladly
das Gerölle	boulders/detritus
die Gerste	barley

die Gerte	switch/whip
der Geruch, Gerüche	smell, smells
das Gerümpel	junk
das Gerüst	scaffold
gesamt, die Gesamtheit	total, totality/entire, entirety
der Gesang, Gesänge	singing, songs
das Geschäft, geschäftlich	business, business
geschehen, geschah, es geschieht	to happen, happened, happens
gescheit	bright/intelligent
das Geschehen	happening
die Geschichte	history/story
das Geschick, geschickt, die Geschicklichkeit	aptness, apt, aptitude/skill, skillful, skillfulness
das Geschirr	dishes
der Geschmack, Geschmäcke, geschmacklos, geschmackvoll	taste, tastes, tasteless, tasteful
das Geschöpf	creature
das Geschoß, Geschosse	floor, floors (of a building)
das Geschütz	cannon/piece of artillery
das Geschwätz, geschwätzig	gossip, gossipy
geschwind, die Geschwindigkeit	speedy, speed
die Geschwister, Geschwisterkind	siblings, first cousin
der Geschworene	juror
die Geschwülst, -schwülste	tumor, tumors
das Geschwür	ulcer
der Geselle	journeyman/young man who has completed an apprenticeship
die Gesellschaft	society
das Gesetz, gesetzlich	law, legal
das Gesicht	face
das Gesindel	rabble
das Gespann	team/horse and cart
das Gespenst	ghost
das Gespinst	cocoon
das Gespräch	conversation
gesprenkelt	speckled
die Gestalt	figure/shape/gestalt
das Geständnis, nisse	confession, confessions
der Gestank	stench
gestehen, -stand, -standen	to confess, confessed, confessed
das Gestell	rack/support/framework
gestern, gestrig	yesterday, yesterday's
das Gestirn	celestial body
das Gesträuch	shrubbery
das Gestrüpp	brushwood
gesund, die Gesundheit	healthy, health
das Getränk	drink/beverage
das Getreide	grain
getrost	confidently/easily
das Getümmel	hubbub
der Gevatter, Gevatterin, -innen	godfather, godmother, godmothers
das Gewächs	plant/growth
gewahr werden	to become aware of
die Gewalt, gewaltig	force/strength/violence, powerful/mighty/terrific
das Gewand, Gewänder	garment, garments
das Gewehr	gun/rifle
das Geweih, Geweihe	antlers (sg. & pl.)
das Gewerbe	trade/small business
das Gewicht	weight
der Gewinn, der Gewinst	profit, return
gewinnen, gewann, gewonnen	to win, won, won
gewiß, gewisser	certain, sure
das Gewissen, gewissenhaft	conscience, conscientious
das Gewitter, es gewittert	thunderstorm, it thunders
gewöhnen, gewöhnt	to accustom so. to, accustomed/to get used to, being used to
die Gewohnheit	custom/habit/practice
gewöhnlich	common/ordinary
das Gewölbe	vaulting
das Gewölk	clouds
das Gewürz	spice
die Gicht, gichtisch	gout, gout-ridden
der Giebel	gable
die Gier, gierig	greed, greedy
gießen, goß, gegossen	to pour, poured, poured
das Gift, giftig, giften	poison, poisonous, to poison
das Gilet = die Weste	gilet = vest
der Gimpel	bullfinch
der Gipfel = Berggipfel	summit = mountain top
der Gips	plaster
die Gitarre	guitar
das Gitter	grate/grid
der Glanz, glänzen, glänzend	shine, to shine, shiny
das Glas, Gläser, gläsern	glass, glasses, glassy
der Glaser	glazier

glasieren, die Glasur	to glaze, glaze
glatt	flat/smooth
die Glätte, glätten	smoothness, to smooth
die Glatze, glatzköpfig	bald head, bald
der Glaube, glauben, gläubig	belief, to believe, believing/ devout
gleich	equal
gleichen, glich, geglichen	to equal, equaled, equaled/ to resemble, resembled, resembled
gleichförmig	homogenous/uniform
das Gleichgewicht	equilibrium
gleichgültig	indifferent
gleichmäßig	steady/regular/proportional
das Gleichnis, -nisse	parable, parables/allegory, allegories
gleichsam	quasi/as it were
gleichzeitig	simultaneously
das Gleis = Geleise	track = tracks (of a train)
gleiten, glitt, geglitten	to glide, glided, glided
der Gletscher	glacier
das Glied	limb
die Gliedmaßen	extremities
glimmen = glühen; glomm, geglommen	to smolder = to glow; glimmered, glimmered
der Glimmer	glimmer
glitschen, glitschig	to slither, slimy
glitzern	to glitter
der Globus, die Globen	globe, globes
die Glocke	bell
das Gloria	glory
glotzen, glotzte, geglotzt	to gawk, gawked, gawked
das Glück, glücklich	fortune, fortunate/happiness, happy
glücken, es glückt	to succeed, succeeded
glückselig	blissful
glühen, glühte, geglüht, die Glut	to glow, glowed, glowed, embers
der Glühwurm, -würmer	firefly, fireflies
die Glut	embers
das Glyzerin	glycerin
die Gnade, gnädig	mercy, merciful/grace, gracious
der Gneis	gneiss
der Gockelhahn, -hähne	cock, cocks
das Gold, golden	gold, golden
die Gondel, gondeln	gondola, to tootle along
gönnen	to treat/to indulge
der Göpel : Pferdegöpel	horse-capstan : horse-gin
gotisch, die Gotik (Baustil)	Gothic, Gothic (building style)
der Gott, Götter, göttlich	God, Gods, divine
Gottlieb	Gottlieb
gottlob!	thank God!
der Götze	idol
das Grab, Gräber	grave, graves
graben, grub, gegraben, du gräbst, gräbt	to dig, dug, dug, you dig, digs
der Graben, Gräben	ditch, ditches
das Grabmal	tomb
das Grabscheit	spade
der Grad, Grade, 3 Grad Wärme	degree, degrees, 3 degrees temperature
der Graf, die Gräfin	count, countess
der Gram, grämlich	sorrow, sullen
das Gramm = Grammgewicht	gram = gram in weight
das Grammophon	gramophone
die Granate	grenade
der Granit	granite
der Graphit	graphite
das Gras, Gräser, grasen	grass, grasses, to graze
gräßlich	dreadful
der Grat = Schneide eines Berges	ridge = crest of a mountain
die Gräte = Fischgräte	fishbone
gratis	free of charge
grätschen, die Grätsche	to straddle, straddle
gratulieren, die Gratulation	to congratulate, congratulations
grau	grey
die Graupe	hulled barley
graupeln	to sleet
grausam, die Grausamkeit	cruel, cruelty
grauslich	ghastly
graziös	graceful
greifen, griff, gegriffen	to grip, gripped, gripped
greinen	to whine
der Greis, die Greisin, -innen	old man, old woman, old women
der Greisler	grocer
grell	garish
die Grenze, angrenzen	border, to border
Grete, Gretel	Margerita, Margery
greulich	greyish
der Grieche, griechisch, Griechenland	the Greek, Greek, Greece
der Grieß, Grießmehl	semolina, semolina/farina

der Griff	grip/handle	der Gusto = Lust	gusto = desire
der Griffel	stylus	gut, besser, am besten	good, better, best
die Grille	cricket	das Gut, Güter	goods/property, goods/properties
der Grimm, grimmig	grim, grim	die Güte	mercy
der Grind, grindig	scab, scabby	gutmütig	kindhearted/good-humored
grinsen	to grin	das Gymnasium, Gymnasien, der Gymnasiast	high school, high schools, high school student
die Grippe (Krankheit)	flu (illness)		
grob, gröber, am gröbsten, die Grobheit, der Grobian	coarse, coarser, coarsest, coarseness, ruffian		
der Groll, grollen	wrath, to grumble	das Haar, haarig, das Härchen	hair, hairy, tiny hair
groß, größer, am größten, die Größe	big, bigger, biggest, stature/size	haben, hatte, gehabt, du hast, er hat	to have, had, had, you have, he has
großartig, großmütig	magnificent, magnanimous	die Habgier, habgierig	greed, greedy
der Groschen	penny	der Habicht	hawk
die Grotte	grotto	die Habsucht, habsüchtig	covetousness, covetous
die Grube	pit	die Hacke, hacken	hoe (garden tool), to hack
grübeln, der Grübler	to ponder, ponderer	der Häcksel, der Häcker-ling	chaff cutter, chaff
die Gruft, Grüfte	crypt, crypts	der Hader	strife/rags
das Grummet	aftergrass	der Hafen, Häfen	harbor, harbors
grün, im Grünen, grünen, es grünt	green, in the countryside, to turn green/to flourish, it turns green/it flourishes	der Hafer	oats
		das Häferl = Töpfchen	mug = little pot
der Grund, die Gründe	reason/ground/land, reasons/grounds	der Hafner	stove fitter
		die Haft	imprisonment
gründen, der Gründer	to found, founder	das Haftel	hook
gründlich, die Gründlichkeit	thorough, thoroughness	haften	to be liable/to adhere
der Grundriß, -risse	floor plan, floor plans	der Hagel, hageln, es hagelt	hail, to hail, it hails
grünen, es grünt	to sprout, it is sprouting	der Hahn, Hähne	rooster, roosters
der Grünspan	verdigris/copper rust	häkeln, die Häkelei	to crochet, crocheting
grünen	to turn green/to flourish	der Haken, das Häkchen	hook, hooklet
die Gruppe, gruppieren	group, to group	halb, halbieren	half, to halve
der Gruß, Grüße	greeting, greetings	die Halbscheid	half
gruseln, gruselig	to give so. the creeps, creepy	halbwegs	halfway
grüßen, grüßte, gegrüsst, du grüßt, grüß Gott!	to greet, greeted, greeted, you greet, good day!	die Hälfte	half
		die Halle	hall
gucken, der Gucker	to look, field glasses	halleluja!	hallelujah!
der Gugelhupf	Bundt cake	hallen, es hallt	to echo, it echoes
das Gulasch	goulash	hallo!	hello!
gültig, die Gültigkeit	valid, validity	der Halm	blade (of grass)
der Gummi, gummieren	rubber/gum, to rubberize/to gum	der Hals, Hälse	throat, throats
		der Halt, den Halt verlieren, halt!	support, to lose one's footing, stop!
günstig	convenient/favorable	haltbar	durable
die Gurgel, gurgeln	throat, to gurgle	halten, hielt, gehalten, du hältst, er hält	to hold, held, held, you hold, he holds/to last, lasted, lasted, you last, he lasts/to stop, stopped, stopped, you stop, he stops
die Gurke, Essiggurke	cucumber, pickle		
der Gurt, die Gurte	strap, straps		
der Gürtel, gürten	belt, to belt		
der Guß, des Gusses, Güsse	cast, of the cast, casts		

die Haltung	attitude
der Halunke	scoundrel
der Hammel, Hämmel	mutton, muttons
der Hammer, Hämmer, hämmern	hammer, hammers, to hammer
der Hampelmann	jumping jack
der Hamster, hamstern	hamster, to hoard
die Hand, Hände	hand, hands
der Handel, handeln	trade, to trade
der Handgriff	handle
der Händler	merchant, tradesperson
die Handlung	act
der Handschuh	glove
das Handwerk	craft
der Hanf	hemp
der Hang, Hänge	slope, slopes
hängen : angehängt sein; der Hut hängt am Haken, hing, gehangen	to hang : to be hung up/ to be attached; the hat hangs on the hook, hung, hung
hängen : anhängen; ich hänge den Hut auf, hängte, gehängt	to hang : to hang up/to attach; I hang up the hat, hung, hung
Hanna	Hannah
Hans, Hänschen, Hansel	Hans, Johnny, Hansel
das Hantel	dumbbell (for gymnastics)
hantieren	to handle
die Harfe	harp
harmlos	harmless
die Harmonika	harmonica
das Harmonium	harmonium
der Harn	urine
der Harnisch	harness
hart, härter, die Härte, härten	hard, harder, hardness, to harden
das Harz, harzig	resin, resinous
der Haß (von hassen)	hate (from to hate)
haschen	to snatch
der Hase	hare
die Haselnuß, -nüsse	hazelnut, hazelnuts
häßlich	ugly
die Haspel, haspeln	winder/reel, to wind/ to reel
hassen, haßte, gehaßt	to hate, hated, hated
die Hast, hastig, hasten	hurry, hurried, to hurry
die Haube, das Häubchen	bonnet, little bonnet
der Hauch, hauchen	breath/aspirate, to breath/ to aspirate
hauen, hieb, gehauen, du haust, er haut	to strike, struck, struck, you strike, he strikes
der Haufe, anhäufen	pile, to pile
häufig	often
das Haupt, Häupter, Hauptsache, hauptsächlich, Hauptstadt, Hauptwort	head, heads, main thing, mainly, capital city, noun
das Haus, Häuser, häuslich, das Häuschen, der Häusler, haushalten, zu Hause	house, houses, homey, little house, householder/ cottager, to keep house, at home
hausen, hauste, gehaust	to live, lived, lived/to economize, economized, economized
hausieren, der Hausierer	to peddle, peddler
die Haut, Häute, häuten	skin, skins, to skin
die Hebamme	midwife
der Hebel	lever
heben, hob, gehoben	to lift, lifted, lifted
der Heber	lifter
die Hecke	hedge
der Hederich	wild radish
Hedwig	Hedwig
das Heer (Soldaten)	army (soldiers)
die Hefe = Germ	yeast
das Heft	notebook
heften	to staple
heftig, die Heftigkeit	fierce, fierceness/vehement, vehemence
hegen, der Heger	to foster, wildlife manager
die Heide, Heidekraut	heath, heather
die Heidelbeere	huckleberry/blueberry
heikel, heiklig	delicate, touchy
das Heil, heil, heilen, die Heilung	well-being, healed, to heal, healing
der Heiland	Savior
heilig, der Heilige, Heiligenbild	sacred, saint, picture of a saint/icon
das Heim, heim gehen, heimfahren	home, to go home, coming home
die Heimat	homeland
heimlich	secret
heimwärts	homewards
das Heimweh	homesickness
Heinrich	Heinrich
die Heirat, heiraten	wedding, to wed
heiß, heißer, am heißesten	hot, hotter, hottest
heißen, hieß, geheißen, du heißt	to be called, was called, has been called, you are called
heiser, die Heiserkeit	hoarse, hoarseness
heiter, die Heiterkeit	cheerful, cheerfulness

heizen, heizte, geheizt, du heizt, der Heizer, die Heizung	to heat, heated, heated, you heat, heater, heating/ furnace
das Hektar = ha	hectare = ha
der Hektoliter = hl	hectoliter = hl
der Held	hero
helfen, half, geholfen, du hilfst, hilft, hilf! der Helfer, die Hilfe	to help, helped, helped, you help, helps, help!, helper, help
hell, die Helle oder die Helligkeit	bright, brightness or light
der Helm	helmet
das Hemd, die Hemden	shirt, shirts
hemmen, die Hemmung	to inhibit, inhibition
der Hemmschuh	skid/stop block
der Hengst	stallion
der Henkel	handle (of a cup or a bag)
her, hin und her	towards/ago/here/from, back and forth
herab, heran, herauf	down, close, upstairs
heraus	out
heraußen	outside
herb	acerbic/tart
herbei	here/hither
der Herbst, herbstlich	autumn, autumnal
die Herbstzeitlose	autumn crocus
der Herd	stove
die Herde, Schafherde	flock, flock of sheep
herein	come in
Hermann	Herman
Hermine	Hermine
hernach	hereafter
der Herr, Herr Lehrer	Mr./gentleman, Mr. Teacher
der Herrgott	God
herrlich, die Herrlichkeit	glorious, glory
die Herrschaft, herrschaftlich	reign/rule, stately
herrichten, der Herrichter	to prepare, preparer
herstellen, hergestellt	to manufacture, manufactured
herüber	over/across
herum	around
herunter	downward
hervor	forth
das Herz, das Herzklopfen	heart, palpitations
herzig	adorable/cute
herzlich, die Herzlichkeit	cordial, cordiality
der Herzog, das Herzogtum	duke, duchy
die Hetze, hetzen, hetzte, gehetzt	rush, to rush, rushed, rushed
das Heu, Heuernte	hay, hay harvest
heucheln, der Heuchler	to feign/to be a hypocrite, hypocrite
heuer	this year
heulen	to bawl
heurig, heurige Erdäpfel, der Heurige (Wein)	this year's, early potatoes, new wine
die Heuschrecke	grasshopper
heute, Heute abend, heutig	today, tonight, today's
die Hexe, die Hexerei	witch, witchcraft
der Hexenschuß	lumbago
der Hieb	blow/strike
hier	here
hierauf	hereupon
hierher	here/hither
hierhin	here/hither
hiesig	local
Hilda	Hilda
Hilfe, zu Hilfe	help, (came) to help
hilflos	helpless
die Himbeere	raspberry
Himmel, Himmelfahrt	heaven, Ascension
die Himmelschlüssel	cowslip primrose
hin, hin und her	towards, back and forth
hinab, hinauf, hinaus	downstairs, upstairs, out
hindern, das Hindernis, -nisse	to hinder, obstacle, obstacles
hinein	into
hinken	to limp
hinten	behind
hinter, hinterher	back, after
hintereinander	consecutively
hinterlassen, -ließ, -lässt	to bequeath, bequeathed bequeathed
hinterlistig	deceitful
hinterrücks	from behind/behind one's back
hinüber	across
hinum	around
hinunter	downstairs
das Hirn	brain
der Hirsch	stag
die Hirse	millet
der Hirt	shepherd
die Hitze	heat
hitzig	heated

der Hobel, hobeln	plane, to plane
hoch, höher, am höchsten	high, higher, highest
die Hochachtung, hochachtungsvoll	respect, respectfully
hochdeutsch	high German
der Hochmut, hochmütig	arrogance, arrogant
höchst, höchstens	most, at most
die Hochzeit	wedding
hocken	to squat
der Höcker, höckerig	hump, humpbacked
der Hof, Höfe	farm, farms
hoffen, die Hoffnung, hoffentlich	to hope, hope, hopefully
höflich, die Höflichkeit	polite, politeness
der Hofrat, Hofräte	court counselor, court counselors
die Höhe	height
höher	higher
hohl : leer; die Höhlung, Hohlraum	hollow : empty; hollow, hollow space
die Höhle, höhlen = aushöhlen	cave/den, to hollow = to excavate
das Hohlmaß, Hohlmasse	measure of capacity, measures of capacity
der Hohn, höhnen, höhnisch	mockery, to mock, mocking
holen = bringen; holte, geholt, hol mir …!	to get = to bring; got, got/gotten, get me …!
der Holer, der Holunder	elder, elderberry bush
Holland, der Holländer, holländisch	Netherlands, Dutchman, Dutch
die Hölle, Himmel und Hölle, höllisch	hell, heaven and hell, hellish
holpern, holprig	to jolt/to jog, bumpy
der Holunder	elderberry bush
das Holz, Hölzer, holzen, hölzern, holzig	wood, woods, to cut down trees, wooden, woody
der Holzschnitt	woodcut
der Honig	honey
der Hopfen	hops
horchen, der Horcher	to listen, listener
hören, der Hörer, das Gehör	to hear, hearer/receiver, hearing
der Horizont, horizontal	horizon, horizontal
das Horn, Hörner	horn, horns
die Hornis, -nisse	hornet, hornets
der Hornist = Hornbläser	hornist = horn player
der Horst	aerie
der Hort	shelter/treasure
die Hose, das Höschen	pants, panties
die Hostie	Host (as of the Eucharist)
das Hotel, der Hotelier	hotel, hotelier
hübsch	pretty
hudeln	to be (too) hasty/to bungle
der Huf, Hufeisen	hoof, horseshoe
die Hüfte	hip
der Hügel, hügelig	hill, hilly
das Huhn, Hühner	chicken, chickens
das Hühnerauge	corn/callus
die Hülle, hüllen, einhüllen	case, to wrap, to enwrap
die Hülse, Hülsenfrüchte	husk, pulses
die Hummel	bumblebee
der Humor	humor
humpeln	to hobble
der Humus	humus
der Hund, die Hündin, -innen, Hundstage	dog, bitch (she-dog), bitches, dog days (of summer)
hundert, das Hundert: viele Hunderte; hundertste, hundertmal, der Hunderter, das Hundertstel	hundred, the hundred: many hundreds; hundredth, hundred times, the hundred, one hundredth
der Hunger, hungern, Hungersnot	hunger, to hunger, famine
hüpfen	to hop
hurra!	hurray!
hurtig	brisk
huschen	to scurry
der Husten, husten	cough, to cough
der Hut, Hüte	hat, hats
hüten, Vieh hüten	to herd, to herd cattle
die Hutsche, hutschen	swing, to swing
die Hütte	hut
der Hydrant	hydrant
die Hymne	hymn
die Hypotenuse	hypotenuse

I

ich	I
Ida	Ida
ideal, der Idealist	ideal, idealist
die Idee	idea
der Igel	hedgehog
Ignaz	Ignace
ihm, in der Mundart: „eam", z. B.: „I hob m g'sagt …"	him (dative case), in dialect: "I have told him…"
ihn, in der Mundart: „n" oder „m", z. B.: „I hob m g'sehn"	him (accusative case), in dialect: "I have seen him."

ihnen, in der Mundart: „eana", z. B.: „I hob's eana g'sogt"	them/you (dative case), in dialect: "I have told you"
ihr, ihres, ihrem, ihren, ihre, ihrer, ihrige	her, hers, their, theirs (inflected)
ihretwegen	because of her
die Illumination, illuminieren	illumination, to illuminate
die Illustration, illustrieren	illustration, to illustrate
der Iltis, -isse	polecat, polecats
im = in dem, in der Mundart: „in", z. B.: „I woar in Zimmer"; im voraus	in = in the, in dialect: "I was in the room"; in advance
der Imbiß, Imbisse	snack, snacks
die Imitation	imitation
der Imker	beekeeper
immer	always
immerhin	anyway
immerwährend	everlasting
impertinent, die Impertinenz	impertinent, impertinence
impfen, die Impfung	to vaccinate, vaccination
der Import, der Importeur, importieren, importiert	import, importer, to import, imported
imprägnieren	to impregnate
imstande sein	to be able
in, in der Mundart: „in", z. B.: „I geh in d' Schul"	in, into, to, in dialect: "I go to the school."
inbrünstig	fervent
indem, indessen	as, however
der Inder	Indian
der Indianer, indianisch	Native American, Native American
Indien, indisch	India, indian
das Individuum, Individuen	individual, individuals
die Induktion, der Induktor	induction, inductor
die Industrie, der Industrielle	industry, industrialist
ineinander	into one another
infam, die Infamie	infamous, infamy
die Infanterie, der Infanterist	infantry, foot soldier
die Infektion, infizieren	infection, to infect
die Influenza	influenza
infolge, infolgedessen	as a consequence of, therefore
der Ingenieur	engineer
der Inhaber	owner
der Inhalt, Inhaltsverzeichnis	content, table of contents
die Injektion	injection

das Inland, inländisch	inland, domestic
innen : drinnen; von innen zusperren	in : inside; to lock from inside
innere, das Innere	inner, inside
innerhalb, innerlich	within, inwardly
innig, die Innigkeit	intimate, intimacy
die Innung	guild
ins = in das	in the/into the/to the
die Inschrift	inscription
das Insekt	insect
die Insel	island
das Inselt = Unschlitt	tallow
insofern	insofar as
der Inspektor, die Inspektion	inspector, inspection
inspizieren	to inspect
der Installateur, Installation, installieren	plumber, installation, to install
inständig	imploring/urgent
der Instinkt	instinct
das Institut	institute
das Instrument	instrument
intakt = unversehrt	intact = unscathed
intelligent, die Intelligenz	intelligent, intelligence
interessant, das Interesse (Aufmerksamkeit, Teilnahme), interessieren	interesting, interest (attention, participation), to interest
intern, das Internat	in-house, boarding school
international (auf alle Nationen ausgedehnt)	international (encompassing all nations)
intim = vertraut	intimate = familiar
invalid, der Invalide	invalid, invalid
inwendig	inner/inside
inzwischen	meanwhile
irden, irdenes Geschirr	earthen, crockery
irdisch, unterirdisch	earthly, underground
irgend, irgendeiner	some/any, someone/anyone
irgendwo, irgendwohin	somewhere, anywhere
irren, irrte, geirrt, du irrst dich	to err, erred, erred, you err
der Irrtum, -tümer, irrtümlich	error, errors, erroneously
die Isolation, isolieren	isolation, to isolate
ist, er ist (von sein)	is, he is (from to be)
Italien, der Italiener, italienisch	Italy, the Italian, Italian

ja	yes
die Jacke, das Jäckchen	jacket, camisole

die Jagd, Jagden, jagen, jagte, gejagt, er jagt, sie jagten	hunt, hunts, to hunt, hunted, hunted, he hunts, they hunted
der Jäger, die Jägerei	hunter, huntsmanship
das Jahr, jährlich, Jahrhundert, Jahreszeit, Jahrmarkt	year, yearly, century, season, fun fair
der Jähzorn, jähzornig	hot temper, hot tempered
Jakob	Jacob
der Jammer, jammern	lament, to lament
jämmerlich	lamentable
der Jänner oder Januar	January
Japan, japanisch	Japan, Japanese
jäten, ausjäten	to weed, to weed out
die Jauche	liquid manure
jauchzen	to rejoice
die Jause	a meal consisting of bread, cold cuts and cheese
jawohl	that's right/indeed
je; je mehr, desto besser	per; the more the better
jedenfalls	in any case
jeder, jede, jedes, jedesmal	each (inflected), each time
jedoch	however
jeher, von jeher	always, from the beginning of time
jemals	ever
jemand	somebody
jener, jene, jenes	that (inflected)
jenseits	beyond
der Jesuit	Jesuit
Jesus, Jesus Christus	Jesus, Jesus Christ
jetzig, die jetzige Zeit	present, the present time/ the present day
jetzt	at present/now
das Joch	yoke
das Jod, jodiertes Salz	iodine, iodized salt
jodeln, der Jodler	to yodel, yodeler
Johann, Johannes, Johanna	Johann, Johannes, Johanna
Josef, Josefa, Josefine	Joseph, Josephine, Josephine
der Jubel, jubeln	jubilation, to jubilate
das Jubiläum	anniversary
jucken	to itch
der Jude, jüdisch	Jew, Jewish
die Jugend, jugendlich	youth, youthful
der Juli : Monat	July : month
Julia, Julie, Julius	Julia, Julie, Julius
jung, jünger, am jüngsten	young, younger, youngest
der Junge = Knabe	boy = lad
das Junge = junges Tier	baby animal = young animal
der Jünger	disciple
die Jungfer, die Jungfrau	spinster, virgin
der Junggeselle	bachelor
der Jüngling	youth/young man
jüngst	recently
der Juni : Monat	June : month
der Jupiter : Planet	Jupiter : planet
der Jurist	lawyer
just, justament	just, just
Justine	Justine
die Justiz	judiciary
das Juwel, der Juwelier	jewel, jeweler
der Jux	prank

K

die Kabine	cabin/cubicle
das Kabinett	cabinet
die Kachel, Kachelofen	tile, tile stove
der Käfer	bug
der Kaffee	coffee
der Käfig	cage
kahl, kahlköpfig	bare, bald
der Kahn, Kähne	barge, barges
der Kaiser, die Kaiserin, kaiserlich	emperor, empress, imperial
die Kajüte	cabin (on a ship)
der Kakau	cocoa
das Kalb, Kälber, kalben, kälbern, das Kälberne	calf, calves, to calve, to calve, veal
der Kalender	calendar
das Kali	potash
der Kalk	chalk/calcium carbonate
kalt, kälter, am kältesten-	cold, colder, coldest
die Kälte	cold
das Kamel	camel
der Kamerad, die Kameradin, -innen	comrade, comrade (female), comrades (female)
die Kamille, Kamillentee	chamomile, chamomile tea
der Kamin	chimney
der Kamm, Kämme, kämmen	comb, combs, to comb
die Kammer	chamber
der Kampf, Kämpfe, kämpfen	fight, fights, to fight
der Kanal, Kanäle	canal, canals
die Kanalisation, kanalisieren	canalization, to channel

die Grippe (Krankheit) [flu (illness)]

das Kanapee	canapé
der Kanarienvogel	canary bird
der Kandiszucker	rock candy
das Kaninchen	rabbit
die Kanne	pitcher
der Kanon : Gesang; Kanons	canon : singing; canons
die Kanone : Waffe	cannon : weapon
die Kante, kantig	edge, angular
die Kantine	canteen
die Kanzel	pulpit
die Kanzlei	lawyer's office
der Kanzler	chancellor
der Kapaun	capon
die Kapelle	chapel
der Kapellmeister	conductor (in music)
kapieren = verstehen	to catch on to sth. = to understand
das Kapital, der Kapitalist	capital, capitalist
der Kapitän	captain
das Kapitel	chapter
die Kappe	cap
die Kaprize = Laune; kaprizieren	caprice = mood; to insist on/to focus on
die Kapsel	capsule
kaputt	broken
die Kapuze	hood (of clothing)
der Karabiner	carabiner
das Karbid	carbide
das Karbol	carbolic acid
der Kardinal, Kardinäle	cardinal, cardinals
der Karfiol	cauliflower
der Karfreitag	Good Friday
karieren, kariert	to checker, checkered
die Karikatur	caricature
Karl, Karoline	Carl, Caroline
karminrot	crimson
das Karnickel	rabbit/bunny rabbit
Kärnten, der Kärntner, kärntnerisch	Carinthia, Carinthian, Carinthian
Karoline	Carolina
die Karotte	carrot
der Karpfen	carp
der Karren	cart
der Karsamstag	Holy Saturday
die Karte	map
die Kartoffel	potato
der Karton	cardboard box
das Karussel	carousel
die Karwoche	Holy Week
der Käse	cheese
die Kaserne	barracks
Kaspar	Casper
der Kasperl	Punch
die Kassa, die Kasse	cash register
der Kassier, einkassieren	cashier, to collect
die Kastanie	chestnut
der Kasten	box
der Katalog	catalogue
der Katarrh	catarrh
der Kataster	land registry/property register
der Katechet	catechist
der Katechismus, -ismen	catechism, catechisms
der Kater	tomcat/male cat
Katharina, Katharine	Caterina, Catherine
das Katheder	catheter
die Kathete	leg of a right-angled triangle
der Katholik, katholisch	Catholic, Catholic
der Kattun	calico
die Katze, katzenartig	cat, cat-like
kauen	to chew
kauern	to cower
der Kauf, kaufen	buy, to buy
der Käufer	customer
der Kaufmann	merchant
die Kaulquappe	tadpole
kaum	barely
der Kautschuk	caoutchouc
der Kauz, das Käuzchen	owl, little owl
der Kavalier	cavalier
die Kavallerie, der Kavallerist	cavalry, cavalryman
keck, die Keckheit	cheeky, cheekiness
der Kegel, kegeln = Kegelscheiben, kegelscheiben	bowling pin, to bowl = skittles, to skittle
die Kehle, der Kehlkopf	throat, larynx
kehren	to sweep
der Kehricht	rubbish
keifen	to nag
der Keil, keilen	wedge, to wedge
der Keim, keimen	germ, to germinate

WORD BOOK

kein, keiner, keine, keines	not a, nobody, not any, not any
keinerlei	in no way
keinesfalls	not at all
der Kelch	goblet
die Kelle = Maurerkelle	trowel = brick trowel
der Keller, die Kellerei	cellar, winery
der Kellner, die Kellnerin, -innen	waiter, waitress, waitresses
die Kelter = Weinpresse; keltern	press = wine press; to press sth.
kennen, kannte, gekannt, du kennst, kennt	to know, knew, known, you know, knows
die Kenntnis, -nisse	knowledge (sg. & pl.)
das Kennzeichen	mark (of identification)
die Kerbe, kerben = einschneiden	notch, to notch = to cut into
das Kerbelkraut	chervil
der Kerker	dungeon
der Kerl	guy
der Kern	pit (of fruit)
die Kerze	candle
der Kessel	kettle
die Keste = Kastanie	chestnut
die Kette, anketten	chain, to chain
keuchen, der Keuchhusten	to wheeze, whooping cough
die Keule	club/mace
die Keusche	cottage
kichern	to giggle
der Kiebitz, kiebitzen	kibitzer, to kibitz
der Kiefer, Oberkiefer	jaw, upper jaw
die Kiefer = Föhre	pine = Scots pine
der Kiel	keel
die Kieme	gill
der Kien, Kienspan	pine, chips of pinewood
der Kies	gravel
der Kiesel, Kieselstein	pebble, pebblestone
das Kilogramm	kilogram
der Kilometer	kilometer
das Kind, kindisch, kindlich, die Kinderei, Kindsfrau	child, childish, childlike, childish trick, little innocent/nymph
das Kinn	chin
das Kipfel	croissant
kippen	to tip over
die Kirche, kirchlich	church, ecclesiastical
die Kirchweih	parish fair
die Kirsche	cherry
das Kissen = Polster	pillow = cushion

die Kiste	box
der Kitt, kitten = leimen	glue, to glue = to glue together
der Kittel	smock
der Kitzel, kitzeln, kitzlich	tickle, to tickle, ticklish
das Kitzerl = junge Ziege	kid = young goat
die Klafter	cord (of wood)
die Klage, klagen	complaint, to complain
der Kläger	complainant
kläglich	dismal
die Klamm	gorge/ravine
die Klammer, anklammern	clip, to clip
der Klang, Klänge	sound, sounds
die Klappe, klappen	flap, to fold
die Klapper, klappern	rattle, to rattle
der Klaps, Klapse	slap/smack, slaps/smacks
klar, klären, die Klarheit	clear, to clear up, clarity
Klara, Klärchen	Clara, Clairene
die Klarinette, der Klarinettist	clarinet, clarinetist
die Klasse	class
die Klassifikation, klassifizieren	classification, to classify
der Klassiker, klassisch	classic, classical
der Klatsch, klatschen, du klatschst	gossip, to gossip, you gossip
klauben = aufklauben	to pick/to gather = to pick up
die Klaue, Klauenseuche	hoof, foot-and-mouth disease
die Klause	hermitage
das Klavier	piano
kleben, klebrig, Klebstoff	to adhere, sticky, adhesive
der Kleber	adhesive
der Klecks, klecksen	blot, to blotch
der Klee, Kleeblatt	clover, cloverleaf
das Kleid, kleiden	dress, to dress
die Kleidung, Kleidungsstück	clothes, piece of clothing
die Kleie	bran
klein, die Kleinigkeit, Kleingeld	small, a little thing/bagatelle, coins
der Kleister, kleistern	paste, to paste
Klemens	Clemens
klemmen, die Klemme	to clamp, clamp
der Klempner	plumber
der Klepper	nag (horse)
klerikal	clerical
die Klette	burr

64

klettern	to climb	der Knobel = Knoblauch	garlic
klieben = spalten	to cleave = to split	der Knöchel	knuckle
das Klima	climate	der Knochen, knochig	bone, boney
klimpern	to tinkle	der Knödel	dumpling
die Klinge = Messerklinge	blade = blade of a knife	der Knofel = Knoblauch	garlic
die Klingel, klingeln	bell, to ring	die Knolle, knollig	bulb, bulbous
klingen, klang, geklungen, der Klang	to sound, sounded, sounded, sound	der Knopf, Knöpfe, knöpfen	button, buttons, to button
die Klinik (Spital)	clinic (hospital)	der Knorpel, knorpelig	cartilage, cartilaginous
die Klinke : Türklinke	handle : door handle	knorrig	knobby
die Klippe	cliff	die Knospe	bud
klirren	to clatter	der Knoten, knotig	knot, knotty
der Kloben, klobig	chunk, chunky	knüpfen	to knot
klopfen	to knock	der Knüppel	bludgeon
der Klöppel, klöppeln, Klöppelspitze	bobbin, to make bobbin lace, bobbin lace	knurren	to growl
das Klosett	toilet	knuspern	to nibble
das Kloster, Klöster	cloister, cloisters	der Knüttel	cudgel
der Klotz, Klötze	block, blocks	der Kobel	drey
die Kluft, Klüfte	crevice, crevices	der Koben	pen/pigsty
klug, klüger, am klügsten, die Klugheit	intelligent, more intelligent, most intelligent, intelligence	der Kobold	goblin
		der Koch, Köche, die Köchin	cook, cooks, cook (female)
der Klumpen, klumpig	clump, clumpy	kochen, der Kocher	to cook, stove
knabbern	to nibble	der Köcher	quiver
der Knabe = Bub	boy = little boy	die Köchin, -innen	cook (female), cooks (female)
knacken, der Knacker	to crack, cracking tool	das Kochinchinahuhn	cochin-china chicken
die Knackwurst	knackwurst	der Koffer	suitcase
der Knall, knallen	bang, to bang	der Kogel	mountain peak
knapp, die Knappheit	scarce, scarcity	der Kognak	cognac
der Knappe (Ritter)	knave (knight)	der Kohl, Kohlrübe	cabbage, rutabaga
knarren	to creak	die Kohle, verkohlen	coal, to char
der Knaster	tobacco	der Köhler	charcoal burner
knattern	to rattle	die Kohlmeise	great tit
der Knäuel	wad/ball (of wool)	der Kohlrabi	kohlrabi/cabbage turnip
der Knauser, knausern	cheapskate, to skimp	der Koks	coke
knautschen	to crumple	die Kolatsche	yeast pastry with sweet or cheese filling
der Knecht	farm hand		
kneifen, Kniff, gekniffen	to pinch, pinch, pinched	der Kolben	piston
die Kneipe, Kneipen	pub, pubs	der Kollege	colleague
kneten	to knead	kollern	to gobble
der Knick, knicken	kink, to kink	die Kolonie	colony
der Knicks, knicksen	curtsy, to curtsy	das Kolophonium = Geigenharz	colophony = rosin
das Knie, knien, ich knie	knee, to kneel, I kneel	kolossal	colossal
der Knirps	munchkin	der Komet	comet
knistern	to crackle	komisch	funny
knittern, zerknittern	to crease, creased/wrinkled		

der Kommandant, kommandieren, das Kommando	commander, to command, command
kommen, kam, gekommen, du kommst, kommt, komm!	to come, came, come, you come, comes, come!
der Kommis	clerk
der Kommissär, das Kommissariat	commissioner, police station
die Kommission	commission
kommod = bequem	comfortable = convenient
die Kommode = Schubladekasten	bureau = commode
die Kommunion, kommunizieren	communion, to communicate
der Kommunist, kommunistisch	communist, communist
die Komödie	comedy
der Kompagnon	companion
die Kompanie	company (mil.)/business
der Kompaß, Kompasse	compass, compasses
komplett	complete
das Kompliment	compliment
kompliziert = verwickelt	complicated = complex
komponieren, der Komponist	to compose, composer
das Kompott	compote
die Konditorei = Zuckerbäckerei	pastry shop = pastry bakery
der Konduktor = Schaffner	conductor = carman
die Konferenz	conference
die Konfession = Glaubensbekenntnis; konfessionell, konfessionslos	denomination = creed; denominational, nondenominational
konfus, die Konfusion = Verwirrung	confused, confusion = mix-up
der König, die Königin, -innen, königlich	king, queen, queens, royal
konisch = kegelförmig	conical = cone-shaped
die Konkurrenz = Wettbewerb; konkurrieren	competition = rivalry; to compete
können, konnte, gekonnt, ich kann, kannst, könnte	to can, could, could, I can, can, could
Konrad	Conrad
die Konserve	can/canned food
konstruieren	to construct
die Konstruktion (Bau)	construction (building site)
der Konsul, das Konsulat	consul, consulate
der Konsum	consumption
das Konto : Rechnung, Kontos	account : invoice/check, accounts
das Kontor = Kanzlei; der Kontorist	office = law office; office employee/clerk
die Kontrolle, der Kontrollor, kontrollieren	inspection, inspector, to inspect
konzentriert	focused
das Konzept : Entwurf; Konzeptpapier	concept : outline; draft/proposal
das Konzert	concert
der Kooperator	Catholic curate
der Kopf, Köpfe, kopfüber	head, heads, headfirst
das Kopfweh	headache
kopieren = durchschreiben, nachmachen	to copy = to make a copy, to imitate
die Koralle	coral
der Korb, Körbe, das Körbchen	basket, baskets, little basket
der Kork	cork
das Korn, Körner	grain, grains
der Körper, körperlich	body, bodily
die Korrespondenzkarte, korrespondieren	postcard, to correspond
die Kost	food/diet
kostbar	precious
kosten	to cost
kostspielig	costly
das Kostüm, kostümieren	costume, to get dressed up
der Kot, kotig	feces, fecal
der Kotzen	woolen blanket
krabbeln	to crawl
der Krach, krachen	crash, to crash
das Kracherl	fizzy drink
krächzen	to caw
die Kraft, Kräfte, kräftig	force, forces, forceful
der Kragen, die Kragen	collar, collars
die Krähe	crow
krähen, krähte, gekräht	to crow, crowed, crowed
die Kralle, krallen = kratzen	claw, to claw = to scratch
der Kram, kramen	stuff/clutter, to rummage
der Krämer	grocer
der Krampen	mattock
der Krampf, Krämpfe	cramp, cramps
der Krampus	a companion of Saint Nicholas
der Kran, Kräne	crane, cranes
der Kranich (Vogel)	crane (bird)
krank, kränker, kränklich, die Krankheit	sick, sicker, sickly, sickness
kränken, die Kränkung	to offend, offense
der Kranz, Kränze	wreath, wreaths
der Krapfen	doughnut

WITTGENSTEIN

die Krätze	scabies
kratzen, kratzte, gekratzt, du kratzst, der Kratzer	to scratch, scratched, scratched, you scratch, scratch
die Krause	ruff
kräuseln	to ruffle
das Kraut, Kräuter, krautig	herb, herbs, herbaceous
der Krawall, krawallieren	rumpus, to riot
die Krawatte	tie
die Kraxe (Rückenkorb)	pannier
kraxeln	to clamber
der Krebs, Krebse	crab, crabs
die Kredenz	credenza
die Kreide	chalk
der Kreis, Kreise, kreisen	circle, circles, to circle
kreischen	to screech
der Kreisel	spinning top
die Krempe = Hutkrempe	brim = brim of a hat
der Krempel	junk
krempeln	to roll up
der Kren	horseradish
krepieren = verenden	to die = to perish
das Kreuz, kreuzen, die Kreuzung, kreuzweise	cross, to cross, crossing, crosswise
kreuzigen, die Kreuzigung	to crucify, crucifixion
kriechen, kroch, gekrochen	to crawl, crawled, crawled
der Krieg, Kriegsschiff	war, war ship
kriegen = bekommen	to get = to receive sth.
das Kriminal	penitentiary
die Krippe = Futtertrog	manger = feeding trough
der Kristall, kristallisieren	crystal, to crystallize
kritisieren	to criticize
kritzeln, die Kritzelei	to doodle, doodle
das Krokodil	crocodile
die Krone	crown
der Kropf, Kröpfe, kropfig	goiter, goiters, goitrous
die Kröte	toad
die Krücke	crutch
der Krug, Krüge	pitcher, pitchers
krumm	warped/crooked
krümmen, die Krümmung	to warp, warping
der Krüppel	disabled person
die Kruste	crust
das Kruzifix	crucifix
der Kübel	tub
der Kubikmeter : Raummaß	cubic meter : cubic measure
die Küche	kitchen
der Kuchen	cake
der Kuckuck, Kuckucksuhr	cuckoo, cuckoo clock
die Kufe	skid
die Kugel, kugelförmig	sphere, spherical
kugeln	to roll
die Kuh, Kühe, Kuhhirt	cow, cows, cowherd
kühl, kühlen, die Kühle	cool, to cool, coolness
der Kukuruz	corn
die Kultur	culture
der Kummer	sorrow
kümmern	to take care
das Kummet	horse collar
die Kunde, künden	news, to announce
die Kundgebung	announcement
kündigen, die Kündigung	to give notice, notice
die Kundschaft	clientele
künftig	in the future
die Kunst, Künste	art, arts
der Künstler, künstlich	artist, artificial
das Kunststück	feat/stunt/trick
das Kupfer	copper
die Kuppe = Bergkuppe	top = mountain top
die Kuppel = Kuppeldach	cupola = domed roof
kuppeln = verbinden	to couple = to connect
die Kur, Kurort, kurieren	cure, health resort, to cure
die Kurbel, kurbeln, ankurbeln	crank, to crank, to crank up
der Kürbis, Kürbisse	pumpkin, pumpkins
kurieren = heilen	to cure = to heal
der Kurs	course
der Kurschmied	smithy and horse doctor
Kurt	Kurt
kurz, kürzer, die Kürze	short, shorter, shortness
kürzen	to shorten
kürzlich	recently
der Kurzschluß, Kurzschlüsse	short circuit, short circuits
kurzsichtig	shortsighted
kurzum	in short
der Kuß, Küsse, küssen, küßte, geküßt, du küßt, küß!	kiss, kisses, to kiss, kissed, kissed, you kiss, kiss!
die Küste : Meeresküste	coast : seacoast
der Kutscher, kutschieren	coachman, to drive a horse-drawn carriage

WORD BOOK

die Kutte	cowl
der Kuttelfleck	tripe
das Kuvert = Briefumschlag	envelope = envelope for a letter

L

laben = erfrischen	to refresh (with drinks)
lachen, lächeln	to laugh, to smile
lächerlich	ridiculous
der Lack, lackieren	lacquer/gloss paint, to lacquer
die Lacke	puddle
die Lade	drawer
laden, lud oder ladete, geladen, du lädst oder du ladest, er lädt oder ladet, einladen	to load, loaded, loaded, you load, he loads, to invite
der Laden, Läden	shop, shops
lädieren = verletzen	to damage = to injure
die Ladung	load
die Lage	location
das Lager, lagern	warehouse, to store
lahm, lähmen, die Lähmung	paralyzed, to paralyze, paralysis
der Laib = Brotlaib	loaf = loaf of bread
der Laich = Froschlaich, Fischlaich	spawn = frog spawn, fish spawn
lallen	to slur (as in slurred speech)
lamentieren	to lament
das Lamm, Lämmer	lamb, lambs
die Lampe	lamp
der Lampion, Lampions	Chinese lantern, Chinese lanterns
das Land, Länder, ländlich	country, countries, rural
der Landauer	landau
landen, die Landung	to land, landing (of a ship)
die Landkarte	map
landläufich	commonly
der Ländler	ländler/folk dance/folk dance music
die Landpartie	outing
die Landschaft	landscape
der Landstreicher	vagabond/tramp
der Landtag	state (or regional) parliament
der Landwirt, die Landwirtschaft, landwirtschaftlich	farmer, agriculture, agricultural
lang, länger, am längsten, die Länge	long, longer, longest, length
langen, auslangen	to suffice, to be sufficient
langjährig	longtime
länglich	longish
längs = entlang; längs der Straße	along = alongside; along the street
langsam, die Langsamkeit	slow, slowness
längst = seit langer Zeit	long ago = for a long time
die Lang(e)weile, langweilig, langweilen	boredom, boring, to be bored
langwierig	lengthy
die Lanze	lance
der Lappen	rag
die Lärche = Lärchbaum	larch = larch tree
der Lärm, lärmen	noise, to be noisy
die Larve	larva
lassen, ließ, gelassen, du läßt, er läßt, laß!	to let, let, let, you let, he lets, let!
das Lasso	lasso
die Last	burden
lästern	to slander
lästig	onerous/annoying
das Latein, lateinisch	Latin, Latin
die Laterne	lantern
die Latsche = Legeföhre	dwarf pine = Swiss mountain pine
die Latte	slat
der Latz, Lätze	bib, bibs
lau	mild/lukewarm
das Laub, Laubfrosch	leaves, tree frog
die Laube	arbor
die Lauer, lauern	look-out, to lurk
der Lauf, Läufe	run, runs
laufen, lief, gelaufen, du läufst, läuft, der Läufer	to run, ran, run, you run, runs, runner
die Lauge, auslaugen	solution, to leach out
die Laune, launenhaft, launisch	mood, moody, temperamental
die Laus, Läuse, Lausbub	louse, lice, imp
lauschen	to eavesdrop
laut, der Laut	loud, sound
läuten, läutete	to ring, rang
lauter	many
der Lavendel	lavender
das Lavoir = Waschbecken	washbasin = washbowl
die Lawine	avalanche
das Leben, leben, lebendig, die Lebendigkeit	life, to live, lively, liveliness
die Leber, Leberwurst	liver, liverwurst
lebhaft, die Lebhaftigkeit	vivacious, vivacity
der Lebkuchen	gingerbread

der Lebtag, mein Lebtag	life, in all my life
der Lebzelten, der Lebzelter	gingerbread, gingerbread baker
die Lecke = Salzlecke	lick = salt lick
lecken (mit der Zunge)	to lick (with the tongue)
das Leder, ledern = aus Leder	leather, leathern = of leather
ledig	unmarried
leer, leerer Topf, ausleeren, umleeren	empty, empty pot, to empty, to empty out
legen, niederlegen, legte, gelegt	to lay, to lay down, laid, laid
das Lehen	fiefdom
der Lehm, lehmig	loam/clay, loamy/clayey
die Lehne	backrest
lehnen, anlehnen	to lean, to lean on
die Lehre, in die Lehre gehen	apprenticeship, to be an apprentice to so.
lehren = unterrichten; lehrte, gelehrt	to teach = to instruct; taught, taught
der Lehrer, die Lehrerin, -innen	teacher (male),teacher (female)/schoolmistress, teachers (female)
der Lehrling, der Lehrbub	apprentice, trainee
der Leib = Körper	body
das Leibchen : Kleidungsstück	bodice : piece of clothing
leibhaftig	incarnate/real
das Leibschneiden	stomachache
die Leiche, das Leichenbegängnis, -nisse	dead body, funeral, funerals
der Leichnam	corpse
leicht, die Leichtigkeit	light/easy, lightness/ease
der Leichtsinn, leichtsinnig	carelessness/frivolity, careless/frivolous
leid, es ist mir leid, es tut mir leid, das Leid	unpleasant, I'm tired of, I'm sorry, affliction/harm
leiden, litt, gelitten, das Leiden = Krankheit	to suffer, suffered, suffered, suffering = illness
die Leidenschaft, leidenschaftlich	passion, passionate
leider, leider Gottes!	unfortunately, I'm afraid so!
die Leier, leiern	lyre, to play the lyre
leihen, lieh, geliehen, ich leihe, leihst, leiht, leih!	to borrow, borrowed, borrowed, I borrow, you borrow, borrows, borrow!/ to lend, lent, lent, I lend, you lend, lends, lend!
leihweise	as a loan
der Leim = Tischlerleim; leimen	glue = joiner's glue; to glue
der Lein	flax
die Leine	leash
das Leinen, leinen = aus Leinwand	linen, linen = made of linen
die Leinwand	canvas
leise	quiet
die Leiste	ledge
der Leisten	last/shoe tree
leiten, die Leitung	to manage, management
die Leite = Abhang	mountain slope = mountain side
leiten = führen; leitete	to lead = to guide; led
der Leiter, Schulleiter	head, principal (of a school)
die Leiter, Leiterwagen	ladder, rack wagon/cart
die Leitung	guidence/direction
die Lende	loin
lenken, der Lenker	to steer, steering wheel
der Lenz	springtime
der Leopard	leopard
Leopold, Leopoldine	Leopold, Leopoldina
die Lerche : Vogel	lark : bird
lernen = erlernen; schreiben lernen	to learn = acquire; to learn to write
lesen, las, gelesen, ich lese, du liest, er liest, lies! der Leser, die Lese	to read, read, read, I read, you read, he reads, read! reader, harvest
leserlich	legible
die Letter	type (for typesetting)
letzte, zum letztenmal, zum letzten Male, der Letzte der Klasse, vorletzte	last, for the last time, for the last time, the last in class, next to last
letzthin	lately
leuchten, der Leuchter	to shine, chandelier
das Leuchtgas	illuminating gas
leugnen	to deny
die Leute	people
der Leutnant	lieutenant
leutselig, die Leutseligkeit	affable, affability
die Libelle	dragonfly
das Licht, licht = hell	light, light = bright
lichterloh	to be ablaze
die Lichtmeß	Candlemas/Groundhog Day
lieb, lieber, am liebsten	dear, dearer, dearest
die Liebe, lieben, geliebt	love, to love, loved
liebenswürdig, die Liebenswürdigkeit	charming/kind, charm/kindness
lieblich	lovely
der Liebling	darling
das Lied (Gesang)	song (singing)
liederlich, die Liederlichkeit	cocky/sloppy, libertinism/sloppiness
der Lieferant	delivery man

liefern, die Lieferung	to deliver, delivery
liegen, lag, gelegen, du liegst, liegt	to lie, lay, lain, you lie, lies
Liese, Liesel	Liza
der Likör	liquor
lila = lilafarbig	purple = colored purple
Lili : Name	Lili : name
die Lilie : Blume	lily : flower
die Limonade	lemonade
die Limone = Zitrone	lemon = lemon
lind	balmy/gentle
die Linde, Lindenholz	linden, linden wood
lindern, die Linderung	to relieve, relief
das Lineal	ruler
die Linie, linieren, einlinig, vierlinig	line, to line, one-lined, four-lined
linke, linkisch, links	left, clumsy, left
das Linoleum	linoleum
die Linse	lens
die Lippe	lip
die List, listig	cunning, cunning
die Liste	list
die Litanei	litany
der Liter	liter
das Lob, loben	praise, to praise
das Loch, Löcher, löcherig, durchlöchert	hole, holes, full of holes, perforated
die Locke, lockig	curl, curly
locken, lockte, gelockt	to lure, lured, lured
locker, lockern, die Lockerung	loose, to loosen, loosening
der Loden, Lodenstoff	loden, loden cloth
lodern	to blaze
der Löffel, löffeln	spoon, to spoon
die Loge, Theaterloge	loge, theater box
logieren = wohnen	to live = to reside
die Lohe : Gerberlohe	bark : tanbark
der Lohn, Löhne	wage, wages
lohnen, belohnen	to be worth doing, to recompense/to reward
die Löhnung	payment (of wages)
das Lokal	pub
die Lokalbahn, Lokalzug	local railroad, commuter train
die Lokomotive	locomotive
der Lorbeer	bay leaf
los, loslassen, laß los!	off/off you go, to let go, let go!
das Los, losen	lot, to draw lots
löschen, löschte, gelöscht	to extinguish, extinguished, extinguished
das Löschpapier	blotting paper
lose = locker	loose
lösen, die Lösung, löslich	to solve, solution, soluble
die Losung	slogan/password
das Lot	plumb bob
löten, der Lötkolben	to solder, soldering iron
lotrecht	perpendicular/plumb
die Lotterie	lottery
lottern, verlottern	to loaf, to go to seed
das Lotto	lotto
der Löwe, die Löwin, -innen	lion, lioness, lionesses
die Lücke = Loch	gap = hole
das Luder	hussy
die Luft, Lüfte, Luftdruck, luftleer, luftdicht	air, breezes, air pressure, airless, airtight
lüften, die Lüftung	to air, airing
die Lüge, lügen, log, gelogen	lie, to lie, lied, lied
der Lügner, Lügnerin, -innen	liar, liar (female), liars (female)
Luise	Louise
die Luke = Dachluke	hatch = skylight
der Lümmel, lümmelhaft, lümmeln	rascal, rude, to slouch
der Lump, die Lumperei, lumpen, gelumpt	bounder, shabby trick, to lead a loose life, led a loose life
der Lumpen = Fetzen; lumpig	rag = scrap/shred; shabby
die Lunge	lung
lungern, herumlungern	to linger, to loiter
die Lunte	fuse
die Lupe	loupe/magnifying glass
die Lust, Lüste, gelüsten	desire, desires, to desire
der Luster	chandelier
lüstern	lustful
lustig, die Lustigkeit	merry, merriment
das Lustspiel	comedy
der Luxus	luxury
das Lysol	Lysol
das Lyzeum, die Lyzeen	lyceum, lyceums

M

machen, der Macher	to make, maker
die Macht, Mächte, mächtig	power, powers, powerful
das Machwerk	sorry effort

das Mädchen, das Mädel	girl, lass
die Made, madig	maggot, maggoty
das Magazin, der Magazineur	warehouse, warehouse keeper
die Magd, Mägde	maid, maids
der Magen, magenleidend	stomach, with stomach trouble
mager, magerer	meager, more meager
das Maggi	lovage
der Magistrat	municipal council
der Magnet, magnetisch, magnetisieren, der Magnetismus	magnet, magnetic, to magnetize, magnetism
die Mahd = das Mähen	hay harvest = mowing
der Mähder = Mäher	reaper = mower
mähen, mähte, gemäht, du mähst, mäht, mäh! der Mäher	to mow, mowed, mowed, you mow, mows, mow! mower
das Mahl = Essen; Mahlzeit, Mittagmahl	meal = fare; mealtime, lunch
mahlen (Mühle), mahlte, gemahlen	to mill (mill), milled, milled
die Mahlzeit	meal
die Mähne	mane
mahnen, die Mahnung	to warn, warning
der Mai, Maibaum	May, Maypole
der Maikäfer	June bug
der Mais = Kukuruz	corn = Indian corn
die Maische, maischen	mash, to mash
die Majestät, majestätisch	majesty, majestic
der Major	major
die Makkaroni	macaroni
das Mal (nicht: Essen), dieses Mal, diesmal, ein anderes Mal, ein andermal, einmal, zweimal, das erstemal, zum ersten Male, jedesmal, ein paarmal, vielmals, oftmals	time, this time, this time, another time, another time, once, twice, the first time, for the first time, every time, a few times, many times, oftentimes
malen (Bild), malte, gemalt	to paint (a picture), painted, painted
der Maler, die Malerei	painter, painting
das Malheur = Unglück, Pech	malheur = bad luck, misfortune
das Malz, malzen	malt, to malt
das Malzeichen	multiplication sign
die Mama	mama
man (nicht: der Mann), das darf man nicht tun	one, you (not: the man), one/you mustn't do that
manche, mancher, manches	some (inflected)
manchmal	sometimes
die Mandel	almond
der Mangel, Mängel, mangeln	lack/flaw, lack/flaws, to lack
die Manier = Benehmen	manner = behavior
der Mann, Männer	man, men
die Mannschaft	team
die Manschette	cuff (of a shirt)
der Mantel, Mäntel	coat, coats
die Mappe	folder
das Märchen, märchenhaft	fairy tale, fairy-tale
der Marder	marten
Margarete	Margarita
die Margarine	margarine
Maria, Marie	Maria, Mary
Marianne	Marianne
die Marille	apricot
marinieren = einsalzen; mariniert	to marinate = to salt sth.; marinated
die Mark, Ostmark	region, Ostmark
das Mark, Knochenmark	marrow, bone marrow
die Marke, Briefmarke	stamp, stamp (of a letter)
markieren = bezeichnen; die Markierung	to mark = to signify/to label; marking
der Markt, Märkte	market, markets
der Marktflecken	small market town
die Marmelade	marmalade
der Marmor, marmorieren	marble, to marble
die Marone = Kastanie	marron = chestnut
der Mars : Planet	Mars : planet
der Marsch, Märsche, marsch!	march, marches, march!
marschieren	to march
die Marter, martern	torment, to torment
das Marterl	shrine
Martin	Martin
der Märtyrer	martyr
der März: Monat	March : month
der Marzipan	marzipan
das Maß, Maße, Maßstab	measure, measures, scale/measuring stick
die Masche	stitch
die Maschine, Maschinerie, Maschinist	machine, machinery, machinist
die Masern	measles
mäßig, die Mäßigkeit	moderate, moderation
die Maske, maskieren	mask, to mask
die Masse = Menge	mass = quantity
massenhaft	massive/enormous
massieren	to massage

massiv	massive
der Mast, Mastbaum	mast, mast (of a boat)
mästen, die Mästung	to fatten, feeding
das Material, Materialien	material, materials
die Mathematik	mathematics
Mathilde	Matilda
die Matratze	mattress
der Matrose	sailor
das Matsch oder Match = Wettspiel (sprich: Mätsch)	match = game
matt, die Mattigkeit	feeble, feebleness
die Matte	mat
Matthäus	Matthew
Matthias	Matt
die Matura	final exam (at high schools)
die Mauer, mauern, der Maurer	wall, to mason, mason
das Maul, Mäuler	mouth, mouths (of an animal)
der Maulwurf, Maulwürfe	mole, moles
der Maurer	mason
die Maus, Mäuse, das Mäuschen, mäuschenstill	mouse, mice, little mouse, as quiet as a mouse
die Mauser = Federwechsel der Vögel; mausern	molt = shedding of feathers; to molt
Max, Maximilian	Max, Maximilian
die Mechanik, der Mechaniker, mechanisch, der Mechanismus	mechanics, mechanic, mechanical, mechanism
meckern	to bleat/to grumble
die Medaille	medal
die Medizin, der Mediziner	medicine, physician
das Meer, Meeresküste	seas, seacoast
das Mehl, Mehlspeise	flour, pastry
mehr, mehrere, mehrmals, die Mehrheit	more, several, several times, majority
meiden, mied, gemieden	to avoid, avoided, avoided
der Meier, die Meierei, Meierhof	tenant farmer, tenant farm, tenant farm
meilenweit	for miles (and miles)
der Meiler = Kohlenmeiler	pile = charcoal pile
mein, meine, meines	mine (inflected)
meinen, die Meinung	to mean, opinion
meinethalben	as far as I'm concerned
meinetwegen	on my account
meinig, meinige, das Meinige	my, my, mine
die Meinung	opinion

die Meise : Vogel	tit : bird
der Meißel, meißeln	chisel, to chisel
meist, die meisten Leute, das meiste, am meisten	most, most people, the most, the most
meistens	mostly
Meister	master
melden, die Meldung	to report, report
melken, melkte, gemelkt oder molk, gemolken, Melkkuh	to milk, milked, milked or milked, milked, dairy cow
die Melodie	melody
die Melone	melon
die Menagerie	menagerie
die Menge	quantity
mengen, vermengen	to mix, to mix up
der Mensch, menschlich	human, human/humane
merken	to notice
das Merkmal	mark/trait
merkwürdig, merkwürdigerweise, die Merkwürdigkeit	strange, strangely enough, oddity
der Mesner	sacristan
die Messe, Meßgewand	Mass, liturgical vestment
messen, maß, gemessen, ich messe, mißt, die Messung	to measure, measured, measured, I measure, you measure, measures, measurement
das Messer	knife
der Messias (der Gesalbte)	Messiah (the Anointed One)
das Messing	brass
der Met : Getränk	alcoholic drink : beverage
das Metall, metallisch	metal, metallic
der Meteor	meteor
das Meter oder der Meter	meter
die Mette = Frühmesse	Matins = Morning Prayer
der Metzger	butcher
meutern	to rebel/to mutiny
der Mezzanin = Zwischenstock	mezzanine = entresol
Michael, Michel	Michael, Mickey
das Mieder	bodice
die Miene = Gesicht	expression = face
die Miete, mieten, vermieten, der Mieter	rent, to rent, to let, tenant
das Mikroskop, mikroskopisch	microscope, microscopic
die Milch, milchig	milk, milky
mild, die Milde	gentle, gentleness
das Militär, militärisch	military, military
die Milliarde	billion

der Millimeter	millimeter
die Million	million
der Millionär	millionaire
Mina	Minna
minder	minor
minderwertig	inferior
mindeste, mindestens	least, at least
die Mine = unterirdischer Gang	mine = subterranean tunnel
das Mineral	mineral
der Minister	minister
der Ministrant, ministrieren	altar boy, to serve mass
die Minute	minute
mir	me (dative case)
miß.... in mißbrauchen, mißfallen, mißtrauisch, das Mißtrauen, die Mißgeburt usw.	ab-, dis- or mis-... in misuse/abuse, displease, distrustful, distrust, miscarriage, etc.
mischen, die Mischung	to mix, mix/mixture
miserabel = elend	miserable = wretched
mißlingen, -lang, -lungen	fail, failed, failed
der Mist	dung
mit, geh mit mir	with, go with me
miteinander	together
mitgehen	to accompany
der Mitlaut	consonant
das Mitleid, mitleidig	compassion, compassionate
mitsamt	together with
der Mittag, Mittagessen, Mittagmahl	noon, lunch, luncheon
die Mitte, mitten drin	middle, in the midst of
mitteilen, die Mitteilung	to report, report/communicate, communication
das Mittel, mittlere	average, middle
das Mittelalter	Middle Ages
mittellos	without means
mittelmäßig	mediocre/moderate
der Mittelpunkt	center
die Mittelschule, Mittelschüler	middle school, middle school student
mitten, mitten drin	in the middle of, in the midst of
die Mitternacht	midnight
mittlere, der mittlere Teil	middle, the middle part
mittlerweile	meanwhile
der Mittwoch	Wednesday
Mitzi (Marie)	Mitzi (Mary)
das Möbel, möblieren, möblierte Zimmer	furniture, to furnish, furnished room

die Mode, modisch	fashion, fashionable
das Modell	model
der Moder, modern = faulen	rot, to rot = to decay
modern : neuartig	modern : new
die Modistin, -innen	milliner (female), milliners (female)
mogeln, der Mogler	to cheat, cheater
mögen, mochte, gemocht, ich mag, möchte	to like, liked, liked, I like, would like
möglich, die Möglichkeit	possible, possibility
möglicherweise	possibly
der Mohn, Mohnblume	poppy, poppy flower
der Mohr : schwarzer Mensch	blackamoor : black person
der Molch	newt
die Molkerei	dairy
der Moment = Augenblick; momentan = augenblicklich	moment = instant; at the moment = instantly
der Monarch, die Monarchie	monarch, monarchy
der Monat, monatlich	month, monthly
der Mönch	monk
der Mond	moon
das Monogramm	monogram
die Monstranz	monstrance
der Montag	Monday
der Monteur, montieren	assembler, to assemble
das Monument = Denkmal	monument = memorial
das Moos, moosig	moss, mossy
der Mops, Möpse	pug, pugs
der Mord, morden, der Mörder	murder, to murder, murderer
morgen = am folgenden Tag, morgen früh	tomorrow = the following day, tomorrow morning
der Morgen, am andern Morgen, morgens	morning, on the next morning, in the morning
das Morgengrauen	dawn
morgig, der morgige Tag	tomorrow, the next day
Moritz	Maurice
morsch	rotten/brittle
der Mörser	mortar (and pestle)
der Mörtel	grout
der Most	fruit juice
der Motor, Motorrad	motor, motorbike
die Motte : Falter	moth : butterfly
die Möwe	seagull
die Mücke	mosquito
mucken	to mutter
müde, die Müdigkeit	tired, fatigues

das Abendmahl (Last Supper)

der Muff	muff
muffig	musty
die Mühe, sich mühen	effort, to make an effort
die Mühle, Mühlbach	mill, millstream
mühselig	arduous
die Mulde	hollow
der Müller, die Müllerin, -innen	miller, miller (female), millers (female)
die Multiplikation, der Multiplikand, Multiplikator	multiplication, multiplicand, multiplier
multiplizieren	to multiply
der Mumps : Krankheit	mumps : illness
der Mund, Münder, mündlich	mouth, mouths, oral
die Mundart	dialect
das Mündel : Kind unter Vormundschaft	ward : child under guardianship
münden, die Mündung	to flow into, mouth (of a river)
mündlich	oral
munter	cheerful/lively
die Münze	coin
mürb	crumbly
murksen	to bungle
murmeln	to murmur
murren, der Murrer	to grumble, mess
die Muschel	seashell/shellfish
das Museum, die Museen	museum, museums
müßig, der Müßiggang	idle, idleness
die Musik, musikalisch, der Musikant	music, musical, musician
musizieren	to make music
der Muskel	muscle
müssen, mußte, gemusst, ich muß, du mußt, müßte	to have to, had to, had to, I have to, you have to, he would have to
das Muster, mustern	patter, to pattern
musterhaft	exemplary
der Mut, mutig	courage, courageous
die Mutter, Mütter, mütterlich, Muttermal	mother, mothers, motherly, birthmark
mutterseelenallein	utterly alone
der Mutwille, mutwillig	wantonness, wanton
die Mütze	cap
das Myriameter	myriameter/distance marker

N

die Nabe = Radnabe	hub = wheel hub
der Nabel	navel
nach	to/after/for
nachhahmen	to imitate
der Nachbar, die Nachbarin, -innen, die Nachbarschaft	neighbor, neighbor (female), neighbors (female), neighborhood
nachdem	after/when
nacheinander	successively
der Nachfolger, nachfolgen	successor, to succeed
nachgeben	to yield/to give in
nachgehen	to pursue
nachgiebig, die Nachgiebigkeit	compliant, compliance
nachher	later/afterwards
nachlassen	to abate
nachlässig, die Nachlässigkeit	negligent, negligence
der Nachmittag, nachmittags	afternoon, in the afternoon
die Nachnahme	cash on delivery
die Nachricht	news
nachschlagen	to look sth. up
die Nachsicht, nachsichtig	lenience, lenient
nächst, nächste, das nächste Mal, nächstesmal, nächstens	next, next, the next time, next time, soon
die Nacht, Nächte, nachts, heute nacht	night, nights, at night, tonight
der Nachteil, nachteilig	disadvantage, disadvantageous
die Nachtigall	nightingale
nächtigen, nächtlich	to spend the night, nocturnal
das Nachtmahl, nachtmahlen	supper, to have supper
nachträglich	subsequent
nackt	nude
die Nadel, Nadelbaum	needle, conifer
der Nagel, Nägel, nageln	nail, nails, to nail
nagen, der Nager, Nagetier	to gnaw, rodent, rodent
nah, nahe, näher, am nächsten, die Nähe	near, near, nearer, nearest, nearness
nähen, nähte, genäht, du nähst, näht, die Näherin, -innen, Nähmaschine, Nähnadel	to sew, sewed, sewn, you sew, sews, seamstress, seamstresses, sewing machine, sewing needle
nähern = nahe kommen	to approach = to come closer
nähren, nährte, genährt	to nurture, nurtured, nurtured
nahrhaft	nourishing
die Nahrung	food/sustenance
die Naht, Nähte	seam, seams
der Name, namens	name, named
der Namenstag	saint's day

namentlich	by name/notably
nämlich	namely
die Narbe	scar
der Narr, narrisch	fool, foolish
naß, nässer, die Nässe	wet, wetter, wetness
naschen, der Näscher, die Näscherei	to nibble, nibbler, nibbling
die Nase, das Näschen	nose, little nose
die Nässe, nässen	wetness, to wet
national, Nationaltracht	national, national costume
das Natron	sodium bicarbonate/baking soda
die Natter	adder
die Natur, natürlich, Naturgeschichte, Naturlehre	nature, natural, natural history, natural science
Nazi (von Ignaz)	Nazi (from Ignace)
der Nebel, neblig	fog, foggy
neben	next to
nebenan, nebenbei	next door, nearby
nebeneinander	side by side
die Nebensache	minor matter
neblig	foggy
nebst, nebstbei	together with, incidentally/besides
necken, die Neckerei	to tease, teasing
der Neffe	nephew
der Neger	negro
nehmen, nahm, genommen, ich nehme, du nimmst, er nimmt, nimm!	to take, took, taken, I take, you take, he takes, take!
der Neid, neiden, beneiden, neidisch	envy, to envy, to envy, envious
neigen, die Neigung	to tilt/to slant, inclination
nein	no
die Nelke	carnation
nennen, nannte, genannt, du nennst	to name, named, named, you name
der Nenner	denominator
der Nerv, Nerven, nervig	nerve, nerves, annoying
nervös, die Nervosität	nervous, nervousness
die Nessel	nettle
das Nest	nest
nett, die Nettigkeit	nice, kindness
netto : ohne Verpackung	net (as in net weight) : without packaging
das Netz	net
netzen, benetzen	to dampen, to moisten
neu, neuer, am neuesten, etwas Neues; nichts Neues	new, newer, newest, something new; nothing new
neuartig	new/novel
neuerlich	anew
neugeboren	newly born
neugierig, die Neugierde	curious, curiosity
die Neuigkeit	news
das Neujahr	New Year
neulich	recently
der Neumond	New Moon
neun, die Neun = der Neuner	nine, the nine = the number nine
neunzehn, neunzig	nineteen, ninety
New York	New York
die Nibelungen	Nibelungs
nicht	not
die Nichte	niece
nichts	nothing
nichtsnutzig	good-for-nothing
das Nickel	nickel
nicken	to nod
nie	never
nieder, niedrig	lower, low
die Niederlage	defeat
Niederösterreich, niederösterreichisch	Lower Austria, lower Austrian
niederträchtig, die Niederträchtigkeit	base, baseness
niedrig	low
niemals	never
niemand	nobody
die Niere	kidney
nießen, nießte, genießt, du nießt	to sneeze, sneezed, sneezed, you sneeze
die Niete	failure (of a person)
Nikolaus, Nikolo	Nicholas, Nicolo
nimmer, nimmermehr	never again, nevermore
nippen	to slip
nirgends	nowhere
die Nische	nook
nisten	to nest
nobel	noble/refined
noch, nochmals	still, once more
die Nocke, Nockerl	gnocchi, small dumpling
die Nonne	nun
der Norden, im Norden, nördlich, Nordost, nordöstlich, Nordwest, nordwestlich, Nordpol	North, in the north, northern, Northeast, northeast, Northwest, northwest, North Pole
nörgeln, der Nörgler	to nag, nagger

normal	normal
die Not, Nöte, Not leiden, es tut not	hardship, hardships, to suffer hardship, there is a need/it is necessary
der Notar	notary
notdürftig	makeshift
die Note	grade/mark (in school)
der Notfall, Notfälle	emergency, emergencies
notieren	to note
nötig	necessary
die Notiz, Notizbuch	note, notebook
die Notwehr	self defense
notwendig, die Notwendigkeit	necessary, necessity
die Novelle (erzählende Dichtung)	short novel (narrative literature)
der November	November
nüchtern, die Nüchternheit	sober, sobriety
die Nudel, nudeln	pasta, to hug so. tight
die Null, Nullpunkt	zero, zero point
numerieren, das Numero	to number, number
die Nummer	number
nun	now
nur	only
die Nuß, Nüsse, Nußbeugel	nut, nuts, nut-filled croissant
die Nüster	nostril (e.g. of a horse)
nutz, zu nichts nutz, nütze	use, to be useless, of use
der Nutzen, nützen, nützte, genützt, du nützt, nützlich	use, to use, used, used, you use, useful

O

ob	if/whether
die Obacht, Obacht geben	attention, to pay attention
das Obdach	shelter
oben	above/at the top
obenan	at the top
obenauf	on top
ober, obere, oberste, zu oberst	upper, upper, top, highest
oberhalb	above
das Obers, Schlagobers	cream, whipped cream
oberschlächtig	overshot
die Oblate	oblate
der Obmann, Obmänner	chairman, chairmen
die Obrigkeit	authorities
das Obst	fruit

der Öbstler, die Öbstlerin, -innen	fruit schnapps, fruit dealer (female), fruit dealers (female)
obwohl, obzwar	although, in spite of the fact that
der Ochs oder Ochse, Ochsen	ox, oxen
der Ocker, ockergelb	ochre, ochre yellow
öde oder öd	desolate
oder	or
der Ofen, Öfen	oven, ovens
offen = nicht geschlossen	open = not closed
offenbar, die Offenbarung	evident, revelation
die Offenheit	openness
offenherzig, die Offenherzigkeit	candid, candor
öffentlich	public
der Offizier	officer
öffnen, die Öffnung	to open, opening
oft, öfter, am öftesten	often, more often, most often
öfters	often
oftmals	oftentimes
ohne	without
ohnedem, ohnedies	anyhow, anyway
ohnehin	in any case
die Ohnmacht, ohnmächtig	unconsciousness, unconscious/helplessness, helpless
das Ohr	ear
das Öhr = Nadelöhr	eye = eye of a needle
die Ohrfeige, jemanden ohrfeigen	slap, to slap so.
der Ökonom, die Ökonomie, ökonomisch	economist, economy, economic
die Oktave	octave
der Oktober	October
das Öl, ölen, die Ölung	oil, to anoint, anointment
die Olive, Olivenöl	olive, olive oil
die Omelette	omelet
der Onkel	uncle
die Oper, die Operette	opera, operetta
die Operation, operieren	operation, to operate
das Opfer, opfern, die Opferung	sacrifice, to sacrifice, immolation
der Optiker	optician
die Orange = Pomeranze	orange = bitter orange
das Orchester	orchestra
der Orden	order (as in religious order)
ordentlich	neat
ordinär = gemein	ordinary = common

77

WORD BOOK

die Ordination, ordinieren	ordination, to ordain
ordnen, die Ordnung, der Ordner	to order/to arrange, order, folder
die Organisation, organisieren, organisiert	organization, to organize, organized
der Organist	organist
die Orgel, orgeln	pipe organ, to play the organ
der Orkan	hurricane
das Ornament, ornamentieren	ornament, to ornament
der Ort, Orte oder Örter, die Ortschaft, ortsüblich	place, places or villages, village, local custom
die Öse	eyelet/grommet
Oskar	Oscar
der Ost, der Osten, im Osten, östlich	East, East, in the East, eastern
die Ostern, österlich	Easter, paschal
Österreich, österreichisch	Austria, Austrian
östlich	eastern
die Otter = Schlange; der Fischotter	adder = snake; old world adder
Otto	Otto
oval	oval
der Ozean	ocean

P

paar, ein paar = einige; ein paar Äpfel	few, a few = some; a few apples
das Paar = zwei, die zusammengehören; ein Paar Schuhe, das Pärchen, paarweise	pair = two that belong together; a pair of shoes, couple, in pairs
die Pacht, pachten, pachtweise, der Pächter	lease, to lease, on lease, leaseholder
der Pack, das Packel	bundle, small parcel
packen, der Packer, die Packerei	to pack, packer, packing
passen	to fit
das Paket	package
der Palast, Paläste	palace, palaces
Palästina	Palestine
der Paletot = Überrock	paletot = overcoat
die Palette	palette
die Palme, Palmkätzchen	palm tree, pussy willow
panieren, paniertes Schnitzel	to coat with egg and breadcrumbs, breaded schnitzel
der Pansen : Magen	paunch : stomach
der Pantoffel, die Pantoffeln	slipper, slippers
pantschen, der Pantscher, Weinpantscher	to water down, person who waters sth. down, person who waters wine down

der Panzer, panzern	tank, to armor
der Papa`	dad
der Papagei	parrot
das Papier	paper
der Papp	mash
die Pappe, Dachpappe	cardboard, roofing board
der Pappendeckel	cardboard/pasteboard
der Paprika	paprika/bell pepper
der Papst, Päpste, päpstlich	Pope, Popes, papal
die Parade	parade
der Paradeisapfel, -äpfel	tomato, tomatoes
das Paradies	paradise
das Paraffin, Paraffinkerze	paraffin, paraffin candle
der Paragraph	paragraph
parallel = gleichlaufend	parallel = synchronous
das Parallelogramm	parallelogram
parat = bereit	ready = prepared
das Pärchen (von Paar)	couple (from pair)
das Parfüm, die Parfümerie, parfümieren	perfume, perfumery, to perfume
parieren = folgen	to obey = to fall into line
der Park	park
das Parkett, Parkettboden	parquet, parquet floor
das Parlament	parliament
die Partei	(political) party
das Parterre = Erdgeschoß; parterre = ebenerdig	first floor = ground floor; on the first floor = ground-level
der Partezettel	obituary notice
die Partie	party/part
der Paß, Pässe, des Passes	passport, passports, of the passport
der Passagier = Reisender	passenger = traveler
passen, paßte, gepaßt, es paßt, paß auf!	to fit, fit, fit, it fits, watch out!
passieren, passiert	to happen, it happens
die Passion	passion
die Pasta, die Paste, Pasten	pasta, pastas, pastes
die Pastille	lozenge
der Pastor	pastor
der Pate, die Patin, -innen	godfather, godmother, godmothers
das Patent, patent = fein, ausgezeichnet; patentieren	patent, splendid = ingenious, great; to patent
der Pater, Patres	father/priest, fathers/priests
der Patient	patient
die Patin, -innen	godmother, godmothers
der Patron	patron

die Patrone, patronieren	cartridge, to patronize
patzen, patzte, gepatzt, du patzt, der Patzer	to blunder, blundered, blundered, you blundered, blunderer
die Pauke, pauken	kettledrum, to play the kettledrum
Paul, Paula, Pauline, Paulus	Paul, Paula, Pauline, Paulus
die Pause	break (as in recess or intermission)
pausen = durchzeichnen	to copy = to trace
pausieren = ausruhen	to pause = to rest
das Pauspapier	tracing paper
das Pech, pechig, ein Pech haben	bad luck, pitch-black, to have bad luck
peinigen, der Peiniger	to torment, tormentor
peinlich	embarrassing
die Peitsche, peitschen	whip, to whip
der Pelz	fur
das Pendel, pendeln, Penduluhr	pendulum, to sway, pendulum clock
die Pension, pensionieren	pension, to retire
das Pensionat	boarding school
Pepi = Josef	Pepi = Joseph
per, per Stück	per, per piece
das Pergament	parchment
die Perle, das Perlmutter	pearl, mother of pearl
der Perpendikel	perpendicular line
der Perron = Bahnsteig	train platform = track
die Person	person
das Personal	staff
persönlich, die Persönlichkeit	personal, personality
die Perücke	wig
die Pest, Pestbäule	plague, canker
Peter	Peter
die Petersilie	parsley
das Petroleum	petroleum
Petrus	Petrus
das Petschaft, petschieren	seal, to seal
der Pfad, Pfadfinder	path, boy scout
der Pfahl, Pfähle	stake, stakes
der Pfaidler, die Pfaidlerei	tailor, notions store
das Pfand, Pfänder, pfänden	pawn, pawns, to pawn
die Pfanne, Pfannkuchen	pan, pancake
die Pfarre, die Pfarrei, der Pfarrer, Pfarramt	parish, parish, priest, parish office
der Pfau	peacock
der Pfeffer, pfeffern, Pfefferkuchen	pepper, to pepper, gingerbread
die Pfeife, pfeifen, ich pfiff, gepfiffen, der Pfiff	whistle, to whistle, I whistled, whistled, sound of a whistle
der Pfeil	arrow
der Pfeiler	pillar
der Pfennig	penny
pferchen, einpferchen	to corral, to pen
das Pferd, zu Pferde	horse, on horseback
der Pfiff	sound of a whistle
pfiffig, die Pfiffigkeit	sharp, sharpness
die Pfingsten	Pentecost
der Pfirsich	peach
die Pflanze, pflanzen, du pflanzt, der Pflanzer	plant, to plant, you plant, planting pin
das Pflaster, pflastern, der Pflasterer	paving, to pave, paver
die Pflaume	plum
die Pflege, pflegen, der Pfleger	care, to take care, caretaker
die Pflicht, pflichttreu	duty, dutiful
der Pflock, Pflöcke	peg, pegs
pflücken = abpflücken	to pick = to pluck
der Pflug, Pflüge, pflügen	plow, plows, to plow
die Pflugschar	plowshare
der Pfosten	post
die Pfote	paw
der Pfriem	awl
der Pfropfen, pfropfen	cork, to cork
pfui!	yuck!
das Pfund	pound
pfuschen, der Pfuscher, die Pfuscherei	to bungle, bungler, botched job
die Pfütze	puddle
die Phantasie, phantasieren	imagination, to imagine
der Pharisäer	Pharisee
Philipp	Philip
der Philister	philistine
der Phosphor	phosphorus
der Photograph, photographieren, die Photographie, photographisch	photographer, to photograph, photography/photograph, photographic
das Piano : Klavier	piano
piano = leise	piano = soft (in music)
pichen = mit Pech verschmieren	to pitch = to cover with tar
picken	to peck
piepsen	to squeak

der Pikkolo = Kellnerjunge	apprentice waiter
der Pilger, pilgern	pilgrim, to make a pilgrimage
die Pille	pill
der Pilot = Lenker	pilot = driver
die Pilote = Pfahl	pile = pole
das Pilsnerbier	pilsner beer
der Pilz	mushroom
der Pinscher oder Pintscher	pinscher
der Pinsel, pinseln	paintbrush, to paint
der Pinzgauer	citizen of the municipality Pinzgau
der Pips : Krankheit	cold : illness
die Pirsch, pirschen	stalk, to stalk
das Pissoir	(public) urinal
die Pistazie	pistachio
die Pistole	pistol
die Plache	canvas
der Plafond = Zimmerdecke	ceiling
die Plage, plagen	plague, to plague
das Plakat, plakatieren	placard, to placard
der Plan, Pläne, planen, planlos	plan, plans, to plan, planless
der Planet	planet
der Planiglob = Weltkarte	planisphere = world map
die Planke	plank
plänkeln, die Plänkelei	to skirmish, skirmish
planlos, planmäßig	planless, planned
plärren = schreien	to bawl = to scream
das Plastilin	Plasticine
die Platane : ein Ahorn	plane tree : maple tree
das Plateau = Hochebene	plateau = tableland
das Platin	platinum
plätschern	to burble
platt drücken	to flatten
die Platte, Herdplatte	plate, hot plate
plätten = bügeln	to press = to iron
die Plattform	platform
der Plattfuß, plattfüßig	flat foot, flat-footed
der Platz, Plätze, Platz machen, Platz nehmen	place, places, to make room for, to take a seat
platzen, zerplatzen	to burst, to explode
der Platzregen	downpour
plaudern, die Plauderei, der Plauderer	to chat, chat, talker
plauschen = plaudern	to gossip = to chat

die Plombe, plombieren	filling/lead seal, to fill (a tooth), to seal
plötzlich	suddenly
plump	clumsy/chubby
plumpsen	to plop
der Plunder	rubbish
plündern, die Plünderung	to plunder, plundering
die Plunze = Blutwurst	black pudding
der Plüsch	plush
die Pneumatik	pneumatics
pochen	to throb/to rap
das Podium	podium
poetisch	poetic
der Pol	pole
der Polarstern	North Star
Poldi = Leopoldine	Poldi = Leopoldine
Polen, polnisch	Poland, Polish
der Polier = Bauführer	foreman = building supervisor
polieren, die Politur	to polish, polish
die Politik, politisch	politics, political
die Politur	polish
die Polizei, polizeilich, polizeiwidrig	police, police, illegal
der Polizist	policeman
der Pollen = Blütenstaub	pollen
polnisch	Polish
der Polster, polstern	cushion, to upholster
poltern	to bluster
der Polyp	polyp
die Pomade	haircream
die Pomeranze = Orange	sour orange = orange
das Pony	pony
die Pore, porös	pore, porous
das Portemonnaie = Geldbörse	purse = wallet
der Portier	porter
die Portion	portion
der Portlandzement	Portland cement
das Porto, portofrei	postage, postage-free
das Porträt, porträtieren	portrait, to portray
Portugal, der Portugiese, portugiesisch	Portugal, the Portuguese, Portuguese
das Porzellan, porzellanen = aus Porzellan : ein porzellanener Teller	porcelain, porcelain = made of porcelain, porcelain plate
die Posaune, posaunen	trombone, to play the trombone
positiv	positive

die Posse	antic
die Post, Postamt, Postbote, postlagernd, postwendend	post, post office, postman, general delivery, by return mail
die Postarbeit	pressing work
der Posten	position
postieren	to position
der Powidel	plum compote
die Pracht, prächtig, prachtvoll	splendor, splendid, magnificent
Prag	Prague
prägen, die Prägung	to emboss, impress/embossing
prahlen = groß tun	to boast = to lay it on thick
der Praktikant	intern
praktisch	practical
der Prälat	prelate
prallen = anstoßen	to bump into = to knock against
die Prämie = Preis; prämiieren, prämiiert, die Prämiierung	premium = prize; to award a prize; to award a prize to, presentation of a prize
die Pranke	paw
präparieren	to prepare
die Prärie	prairie
der Präsident	president
prasseln	to patter
der Prater	Prater
die Praxis	practice
predigen, die Predigt	to preach, sermon
der Preis, anpreisen	reward, to praise
die Preiselbeere	cranberry
preisen, pries, gepriesen, du preist	to reward, rewarded, rewarded, you reward
der Preiskurant = Preisverzeichnung	commodity price circular = price list
prellen	to bounce
die Presse, pressen, presste, gepresst, Presshefe, Presswurst	press, to press, pressed, pressed, compressed yeast, head cheese
pressieren, pressiert	to be urgent, it is urgent
der Preuße, preussisch, Preußen	the Prussian, Prussian, Prussia
prickeln	to tingle
der Priester	priest
prima Qualität = erste Güte	great quality = superior quality
der Primararzt, der Primarius	chief physician, head of a clinic
die Primaware	top-quality goods
die Primel = Schlüsselblume	primrose = cowslip

primitiv = einfach	primitive = simple
die Primzahl	prime number
der Prinz, die Prinzessin, -innen	prince, princess, princesses
das Prisma, Prismen	prism, prisms
privat, der Privatier	private, person of private means
pro... pro Tag, pro-Stück	per... per day, per piece
die Probe, proben	rehearsal, to rehearse
probieren	to try/to taste
das Produkt	product
die Produktion	production
produzieren	to produce
die Profession = Handwerk, Beruf; der Professionist	profession = trade, occupation; skilled tradesman
der Professor	professor
das Profil	profile
der Profit, profitieren	profit, to profit
das Programm	program
der Proletarier : Besitzloser	proletarian : person without property
die Promenade : Weg, Spaziergang	promenade : walk, stroll
der Propeller	propeller
der Prophet, prophezeien, die Prophezeiung	prophet, to prophecy, prophecy
prosit! prost!	cheers! health!
die Protektion	protection
der Protest	protest
der Protestant, protestantisch	Protestant, Protestant
der Protz, protzen, protzig	show-off, to show off, showy
der Proviant	provisions
die Provinz	province
provisorisch	provisional
das Prozent	percent
der Prozeß, -sse, prozessieren	process, processes, to process
die Prozession	procession
prüfen, die Prüfung	to examine, exam
der Prügel, die Prügel, prügeln, die Prügelei	club, beating, to beat up, brawl
prunkvoll	splendid
der Psalm	psalm
das Publikum	public/audience
der Pudel	poodle
der Puder, pudern	face powder, to powder
der Puff, Püffe, puffen	buffet, buffets, to buffet
der Puffer	buffer

der Puls, Pulsader	pulse, artery
das Pult	lectern
das Pulver, pulverisieren	powder, to pulverize
die Pumpe, pumpen	pump, to pump
der Punkt, punktieren	dot/point, to dot/to point
pünktlich, die Pünktlichkeit	punctual, punctuality
der Punsch	punch
die Punze, punzieren	embossing hammer, to emboss
die Pupille	pupil
die Puppe	doll
das Püree	puree
purpurrot	crimson red
der Purzelbaum, -bäume	somersault, somersaults
purzeln	to tumble
die Pustel	pustule
der Putz, putzen, putzte, geputzt, der Putzer	plastering, to plaster, plastered, plastered, plasterer
die Pyramide	pyramid
der pythagoreische Lehrsatz	Pythagorean theorem

Q

der Quader	cuboid/ashlar
das Quadrat, quadratisch, der Quadratmeter	square, square, square meter
quadrieren	to square
quaken	to quack
die Qual, quälen, der Quäler	torment, to torment, tormentor
die Qualität	quality
der Qualm, qualmen	dense smoke, to smoke
die Quantität, das Quantum	quantity, quantum
das Quargel	small round strong cheese
der Quark	curd cheese
die Quart	quart
das Quartett (vierstimmiges Tonstück)	quartet (music for four voices)
das Quartier = Wohnung	quarters = apartment
der Quarz	quartz
die Quaste	tassel
der Quatember	ember day
der Quatsch, quatschig	nonsense, nonsensical
das Quecksilber	mercury
die Quelle, quellen, quoll, gequollen, es quillt, aufquellen lassen	spring (source of water), to gush, gushed, gushed, it swells, to soak (as in beans)

quer, kreuz und quer, quer über, in die Quere	crosswise, crisscross, across, crossways
der Querschnitt	cross-section
quetschen, die Quetsche, die Quetschung	to squeeze, squeezer, contusion
quiecken, quietschen	to squeal, to squeak
die Quint	fifth
der Quirl, quirlen	whisk, to whisk
quitt = ausgeglichen	even = equal
die Quitte : Apfel	quince : apple
die Quittung, quittieren	receipt, to give a receipt
der Quotient	quotient

R

der Rabbiner (jüdischer Prediger, Religionslehrer)	rabbi (Jewish preacher, religious studies teacher)
der Rabe, rabenschwarz	raven, raven-black
rabiat	rough/furious
die Rache, rächen, sich rächen	revenge, to take revenge, to avenge
der Rachen	throat/pharynx
die Rachitis = englische Krankheit, rachitisch	rachitis = English illness, rachitic
der Racker	little rascal
rackern = schinden	to slave away = to drive hard
das Rad, Räder	wheel, wheels
radeln = radfahren, Radfahrer = Radler	to bike = to ride a bike, bicycle rider = biker
radieren, der Radiergummi	to erase, eraser
das Radieschen	radish
der Radioapparat, Radio...	radio apparatus, radio...
der Radler	biker
raffen	to snatch up/to hoard
die Raffinerie	refinery
raffinieren, raffiniert	to refine, sophisticated/artful
ragen, hervorragen	to tower, to protrude
der Rahm, abrahmen	cream, to skim
der Rahmen, einrahmen	frame, to frame
die Raiffeisenkasse (ländliche Sparkasse)	farmer's cooperative bank (rural savings bank)
der Rain = Ackergrenze	unplowed land = field boundary
die Rakete	rocket
rammen = einschlagen	to ram = to smash
die Rampe	ramp
der Rand, Ränder, umranden	border, borders, to engird

der Rang, Ränge	rank, ranks
der Range (Bub)	young rascal (boy)
der Rangierbahnhof	switching yard
die Ranke, ranken	creeper, to creep
ranzig	rancid
rapid = schnell	rapid = quick
der Rappe	black horse
der Rappel, rappeln	mad whim, to rattle
der Raps	rape (plant)
rar, die Rarität	rare, rarity
rasch, rascher, am raschesten	quick, quicker, the quickest
rascheln	to rustle
der Rasen (Gras)	lawn (grass)
rasen = wüten; rasend	to rage = fuming with rage; raging
der Raseur	barber
rasieren, der Rasierer	to shave, shaver
räsonieren = streiten	to grumble = to scold
die Raspel, raspeln	rasp/file, to rasp/to file (as in wood)
die Rasse, rassig	race, purebred
rasseln	to rattle
die Rast, rasten	rest, to rest
das Rastel, Rastelbinder	wire netting, itinerant tinker
der Raster, rastrieren	grid, to draw a grid
rastlos	restless
der Rat, die Ratschläge	advice, pieces of advice
der Rat: Gemeinderat, Nationalrat; Räte	council: municipal council, national council; councils
raten, riet, geraten, du rätst, rät	to advise/to guess, advised/guessed, advised/guessed, you advise/you guess, advises/guesses
die Rate : Zahlung; ratenweise	installment : payment; in installments
das Rathaus	town hall
ratlos	perplexed/to be at a loss
die Ratsche, ratschen	rattle, to rattle
das Rätsel	riddle
die Ratte : Nagetier	rat : rodent
der Raub, rauben, der Räuber, Raubritter, Raubtier	robbery, to rob, robber, robber baron, predator (animal)
der Rauch, rauchen, der Raucher	smoke, to smoke, smoker
räuchern, die Räucherung	to cure, curing (of food)
der Rauchfang, Rauchfänge, Rauchfangkehrer	chimney, chimneys, chimney sweep
die Räude, räudig	scabies/mange, scabby/mangy
die Raufe = Futterraufe	hack = hayrack
raufen, der Raufer, die Rauferei	to scuffle, ruffian, scuffle/brawl
rauh, rauher, am rauhesten, die Rauhigkeit, die Rauheit	rough, rougher, roughest, roughness, coarseness
der Raum, Räume	room, rooms
räumen, einräumen, aufräumen, wegräumen usw., die Räumung	to vacate, to put away, to tidy up, to clear away, clearance
raunzen, der Raunzer	to grouch, grouch
die Raupe	caterpillar
der Rausch, Räusche, berauscht	intoxication, intoxications, intoxicated
rauschen, du rauschst	to swoosh, you swoosh
räuspern	to clear one's throat
die Raute	diamond (as in lozenge or rhombus)
der Rayon (Umkreis, Gebiet), rayonieren, rayoniert	sphere of responsibility (neighborhood, area), to assign a sphere of responsibility, assigned sphere of competence
die Realität, Realitätenbesitzer	reality/real estate, real estate owner
die Realschule, der Realschüler	secondary school, secondary school student
das Reaumur-Thermometer	Reaumur thermometer
die Rebe, Weinrebe	vine, grapevine
der Rebel, rebellisch, rebellieren	rebel, rebellious, to rebel
das Rebhuhn, -hühner	gray partridge, gray partridges
die Rebschnur, -schnüre	vine cord, vine cords
der Rebus, Rebusse	rebus, rebuses
der Rechen, rechen, Heurechen	rake, to rake, hay rake
das Rechenbuch, Rechenheft, Rechenstunde usw.	arithmetic book, arithmetic notebook, arithmetic lesson etc.
rechnen, der Rechner, die Rechnung	to calculate, calculator, calculation
recht : richtig; dir geschieht recht, du hast recht, nichts Rechtes	right : correct; serves you right, you are right, nothing right/nothing much
das Recht	right/justice/the law
rechte, die rechte Hand	right, right hand
das Rechteck, rechteckig	rectangle, rectangular
rechtfertigen, die Rechtfertigung	to justify, justification
rechts, rechtsum!	right, right turn!
der Rechtsanwalt	lawyer
die Rechtschreibung	orthography/spelling
rechtwinkelig	right-angled
rechtzeitig	in time
das Reck	high bar

recken, sich recken	to stretch, to stretch oneself
die Rede, reden	speech, to speak
die Redensart	idiom/phrase/saying
redlich, die Redlichkeit	honest, honesty
der Redner	speaker
reell = ehrlich	realistic = honest
reflektieren, der Reflektor	to reflect, reflector
der Reflex	reflex
die Reform, reformieren	reform, to reform
die Reformation	Reformation
rege, reger Verkehr	busy, busy traffic
die Regel, regeln	rule, to regulate
regelmäßig, die Regelmäßigkeit	regular, regularity
regelrecht	proper
regen = bewegen	to stir = to move
der Regen, Regenbogen	rain, rainbow
der Regent = Herrscher	regent = ruler
regieren, die Regierung, Regierungsrat	to govern, government, councilor
das Regiment	regiment
das Register, registrieren	register, to register
regnen, regnerisch	to rain, rainy
regulieren, die Regulierung	to regulate, regulation
das Reh, Rehe, Rehbock, Rehgeiß	deer, deer, buck, doe
reiben, rieb, gerieben	to rub, rubbed, rubbed
die Reibung	friction
reich, reich und arm	rich, rich and poor
das Reich, Deutsches Reich	empire, German empire
reichen, hinreichen	to suffice, to be sufficient
reichlich	plentiful
reichsdeutsch, der Reichsdeutsche	under the jurisdiction of the German Reich, person under the jurisdiction of the German Reich
der Reichtum, -tümer	wealth, riches
reif, reifen = reif werden	mature, to mature = becoming mature
der Reif : Frost; bereift	hoarfrost : frost; frosted
der Reifen = Ring; ein Rad bereifen	tire = hoop; to put tires on a wheel
der Reigen	round dance
die Reihe, reihen	line, to line up
die Reihenfolge	sequence
der Reiher	heron
der Reim, reimen	rhyme, to rhyme
rein, reinlich	clean, tidy
das Reindl = Pfanne	casserole = pan
reinigen, die Reinigung	to clean, cleaning
reinlich, die Reinlichkeit	clean, cleanness
der Reis, Reissuppe	rice, rice soup
Reißaus nehmen	to take to one's heels
der Reisbesen	birch broom
das Reißbrett	drawing board
die Reise, reisen, reiste, gereist, du reist, der Reisende	travels, to travel, traveled, traveled, you travel, traveler
reißen, riß, gerissen, du reißt, der Riß, das Reißen = Gliederreißen; reißend	to tear, tore, torn, you tear, tear, tearing = rheumatism; raging/torrential
die Reißfeder, Reißschiene, Reißzeug	drawing pen, T-square, drawing instruments
das Reisig	brushwood
reiten, der Reiter	to ride, rider
der Reiz, die Reizung	stimulus, stimulation
reizen, reizbar	to irritate, irritable
reizend, am reizendsten	charming, most charming
der Reizker : Pilz	lactarius : mushroom
die Reklame	advertisement
reklamieren = zurückfordern	to reclaim = to recall/to claim back
rekommandiert = eingeschrieben	registered = inscribed
der Rekord = Höchstleistung	record = highest achievement
das Relief	relief
die Religion, religiös	religion, religious
die Reliquie	holy relic
die Remise	carriage house
rempeln, anrempeln	to barge, to barge into
renken, ausrenken, verrenken usw.	to contort, to dislocate, to twist etc.
rennen, rannte, gerannt, das Rennen = Wettrennen; Rennbahn	to run, ran, ran, racing = race; racetrack
das Rentier	reindeer
renovieren : ausbessern; die Renovierung	to renovate : to improve; renovation
die Rente	pension/retirement
rentieren, es rentiert sich	to be worth it, it is worth it
die Reparatur, reparieren	repair, to repair
der Repetent	repeater (in school)
repetieren = wiederholen	to repeat = to do again
die Republik, der Republikaner, republikanisch	republic, republican, republican
das Requiem = Totenmesse	requiem mass = mass for the dead
reservieren, reserviert	to reserve, reserved

der Rotz (snot)

das Reservoir = Behälter	reservoir = receptacle
Resi (von Theresia)	Resi (from Theresa)
der Respekt	respect
der Rest	rest/leftover
das Restaurant, der Restautateur, die Restauration	restaurant, restaurateur, restoration
die Retorte	retort
retour = zurück; die Retourkarte = Rückfahrkarte	retour = return; roundtrip ticket = return ticket
retten, die Rettung	to rescue, rescue
der Rettich	garden radish
die Reue, reuen, es reut mich, bereuen	repentance, to regret, I regret, to repent
reuten (Wald, Unkraut)	to clear/to uproot (forest, weeds)
die Reuter = Sieb; reutern	hay drying frames = sieve; to sieve hay in a drying frame
das Revier	district/precinct
die Revolution : Umsturz	revolution : overthrow
der Revolver	revolver
das Rezept	recipe/prescription
der Rhein : Fluß	Rhine : river
das Rheuma oder der Rheumatismus, rheumatisch	rheumatism or rheumatism, rheumatic
der Rhombus : Viereck	rhombus : rectangle
die Ribisel	red currant
Richard	Richard
richten	to fix/to judge
der Richter	judge
richtig, die Richtigkeit	correct, correctness
die Richtung	direction
riechen, roch, gerochen	to smell, smelled, smelled
die Riege	gym team
der Riegel, riegeln	bolt, to bolt
der Riemen	strap
der Riese, riesig	giant, gigantic
die Riese = Holzrutsche	chute = timber chute
rieseln	to trickle
riesig	giant
das Rind, Rindfleisch, Rindsbraten, Rindvieh usw.	cow, beef, roast, cattle etc.
die Rinde : Baumrinde	bark : tree bark
der Ring	ring
ringeln	to curl
die Ringelnatter	grass snake
das Ringelspiel	merry-go-round
ringen, rang, gerungen, der Ringkampf	to wrestle, wrestled, wrestled, wrestling match
die Ringlo oder Reineclaude (sprich: Renklod)	greengage
rings, ringsherum	all around, all the way round
die Rinne	gutter
rinnen, rann, geronnen	to run, ran, run (of water)
das Rinnsal	trickle/rivulet
die Rippe	rib
der Riß, Risse	rip, rips
riskieren, das Risiko	to risk, risk
der Rist	instep
der Ritt	ride (on a horse)
der Ritter, ritterlich	knight, knightly
der Ritz, die Ritze	scratch/crack, scratches/cracks
ritzen, ritzte, geritzt, du ritzt	to scratch, scratched, scratched, you scratch
Robert	Robert
röcheln	to wheeze
der Rock, Röcke	skirt/men's jacket, skirts/men's jackets
der Rocken = Spinnrocken	distaff = spinning distaff
die Rodel, rodeln, Rodelbahn	sled, to sled, sled run
der Roggen = Korn	rye = grain
roh, roher, am rohesten, die Roheit	rough, rougher, roughest, roughness
das Rohr, die Röhre	pipe/tube, pipes/tubes
röhren (schreien)	to roar (to bellow)
die Rolle, rollen	roll, to roll
Rom, römisch	Rome, Roman
der Roman	novel
die Rorate	Mass during Advent
das Roß, Rosse, Roßhaar	horse, horses, horsehair
rosa : Farbe	pink/rosy : color
Rosa, Rosalie (Namen)	Rosa, Rosalia (names)
die Rose, das Röschen, rosenrot	rose, little rose, rose-red
die Rosette	rosette
die Rosine	raisin
der Rosmarin	rosemary
der Rost	rust
rosten = verrosten	to rust = to oxidize
rösten = braten	to roast = to fry
rot, rötlich	red, reddish
die Röte, röten	red/glow, to redden/to turn red
der Rotlauf : Krankheit	erysipelas : illness

WITTGENSTEIN

die Rotte	gang/pack (e.g. of wolves)
der Rotz	snot
die Rübe	turnip
der Rubin	ruby
der Ruck, ruckweise	jerk, jerky
rücken, rückte, gerückt	to shift, shifted, shifted
der Rücken	back
die Rückfahrkarte	return ticket
das Rückgrat	spine
die Rückkehr, die Rückkunft	return, comeback
rücklings	backwards
der Rucksack, Rucksäcke	backpack (sg. & pl.)
die Rücksicht, rücksichtslos, die Rücksichtslosigkeit	consideration, inconsiderate, thoughtlessness
rückwärtig, rückwärts	back, backwards
das Rudel	pack
das Ruder, rudern	rudder, to row
Rudolf, Rudi	Rudolf, Rolfe
der Ruf, rufen	call, to call
der Rufname	first name
rügen	to reproach
die Ruhe, ruhen, ruhte, geruht	rest, to rest, rested, rested
ruhig	quiet
der Ruhm, rühmen	renown, to praise
die Ruhr	dysentery/name of a German river
rühren, die Rührung	to stir, emotion
die Ruine	ruin
ruinieren = verderben	to ruin = to spoil
der Rum : Branntwein	rum : spirit
die Rumpelkammer	junk room/storeroom
rumpeln	to rumble/to bump
der Rumpf, Rümpfe	torso (sg. & pl.)
rund, die Rundung, runden, abrunden, rundherum, rundlich, rundum, die Rundschrift	round, roundness, to round, to round off, all around, chubby, all around, round hand
die Runzel, runzeln, runzlig	wrinkle, to frown, wrinkled (of skin)
Rupert, Ruprecht	Rupert, Robert
rupfen	to pluck
der Ruß, rußen, rußig	soot, to smoke/to form soot, sooty
der Russe, russisch, Rußland	the Russian, Russian, Russia
der Rüffel	rebuke
rüsten, die Rüstung	to arm, armor
rüstig	sprightly
die Rute	rod
rutschen, die Rutschbahn	to slide, slide
rütteln	to shake

S

der Saal, Säle	assembly hall (sg. & pl.)
die Saat	sowing/seed
der Sabbat (Samstag)	Sabbath (Saturday)
der Säbel	sabre
das Sacharin : Süßftoff	saccharin : artificial sweetener
die Sache	thing
sächliches Geschlecht	neuter gender
der Sachse, Sachsen, sächsisch	the Saxon, Saxons, Saxon
sachverständig	expert
der Sack, Säcke, das Säckchen	sack, sacks, pouch
säen = anbauen; säte, gesät, ich säe, du säst, sät, Sämachine	to sow = to cultivate/to grow; sowed, sowed, I sow, you sow, sows, sower
der Safran	saffron
der Saft, saftig	juice, juicy
die Sage, sagen, sagte, gesagt	legend/saga, to say, said, said
die Säge, sägen	saw, to saw
die Saison = Hauptzeit	season = high season
die Saite : Darmsaite	string : gut string
das Sakrament	sacrament
die Sakristei	sacristy
der Salamander	salamander
die Salami	salami
der Salat	salad
die Salbe, salben	ointment, to apply ointment
der Salbei : Pflanze	sage : plant
die Saline = Salzwerk	saltery = saltworks
der Salmiak	ammonium chloride
der Salon	salon/drawing room
der Salpeter	saltpeter
die Salve	salvo
das Salz, salzen, salzig, Salzsole	salt, to salt, salty, brine
der Same, die Sämerei	seed, seed shop
sammeln, die Sammlung	to collect, collection
der Samstag	Saturday
samt = mitsamt	along with = including

WORD BOOK

der Samt : Stoff	velvet : fabric
sämtlich	entire
der Sand, sandig	sand, sandy
die Sandale	sandal
sanft, besänftigen	gentle, to appease
die Sanftmut, sanftmütig	gentleness, gentle
der Sänger	singer
Sankt : St. Stephan usw.	Saint : St. Stephen etc.
das Sanktus	Sanctus
die Sardelle	anchovy
die Sardine	sardine
der Sarg, Särge	coffin (sg. & pl.)
der Satan	Satan
satt	full
der Sattel, Sättel, satteln	saddle, saddles, to saddle
sättigen, sättigend	to fill/to satisfy, filling/satisfying
der Sattler	saddler
der Saturn	Saturn
der Satz, Sätze	sentence (sg. & pl.)
die Sau, Säue	sow (sg. & pl.)
sauber, die Sauberkeit, säuberlich	clean, cleanliness, meticulous
säubern, die Säuberung	to clean, cleaning
die Saubohne	fava bean
die Sauce (Soß) : Saft	sauce : juice
sauer, säuerlich, säuern	sour, sourish, to sour
der Sauerampfer	sorrel
der Sauerstoff	oxygen
der Sauerteig	sourdough
saufen, soff, gesoffen, du säufst, er säuft, der Säufer, die Sauferei	to drink, drank, drunk, you drink, he drinks, drunkard, drunken spree
saugen, sog, gesogen, du saugst, saugt	to suck, sucked, sucked, you suck, sucks
säugen, säugte, gesäugt	to suckle, suckled, suckled
das Säugetier	mammal
der Säugling	infant
die Säule	column
der Saum, Säume	seam, seams
säumen	to hem
die Säure	acidity
sausen, säuseln	to whiz, to murmur
die Schabe : Motte	cockroach : moth
schaben	to scrape
schäbig, die Schäbigkeit	shabby, shabbiness
die Schablone	pattern/template

das Schach, Schachspiel, Schachbrett	chess, game of chess, chess board
schachern, der Schacherer	to haggle, haggler
der Schacht, Schächte	shaft, shafts
die Schachtel	box
schade; es ist schade, daß...	pity; it's a pity that...
der Schädel	skull
schaden, der Schaden, Schäden	to damage, damage, damages
schadenfroh	gloating
schadhaft	harmful
schädigen, beschädigen	to harm, to damage
schädlich	detrimental
das Schaf, Schafherde	sheep, flock of sheep
die Schafblattern	chickenpox
das Schaff, das Schaffel	tub, little tub
schaffen = erschaffen; schuf, geschaffen	make = create; made, made
schaffen : anschaffen, fortschaffen; schaffte, geschafft	to get : to acquire, to get rid of; got, gotten
der Schaffner	conductor (on a train etc.)
der Schaft, Schäfte	shaft, shafts
die Schale, schälen	peel, to peel
der Schall, erschallen	sound, to ring out
schalten, einschalten, umschalten	to switch, to switch on, to switch over
der Schalter	counter window/switch
das Schaltjahr	leap year
die Scham, sich schämen	shame, to be ashamed
die Schande, schändlich	disgrace, disgraceful
der Schank	bar/tavern
die Schanze	entrenchment/ski jump
die Schar	crowd/bunch
scharf, schärfer	spicy/sharp, spicier/sharper
die Schärfe, schärfen	spiciness/sharpness, to spice/to sharpen
scharfsinnig	astute
der Scharlach	scarlet/scarlet fever
das Scharnier	hinge
die Schärpe	sash
scharren	to scratch/to paw
die Scharte, schartig	harelip, nicked
der Schatten, schattig	shadow/shade, shady
schattieren, die Schattierung	to shade, shading
der Schatz, Schätze	treasure (sg. & pl.)
schätzen, die Schätzung	to estimate, estimate
der Schauder, schaudern, schauderhaft	shudder, to shudder, ghastly

schauen, schaute, geschaut	to look, looked, looked
der Schauer, schauern, schauerlich	shudder, to shudder, ghastly
die Schaufel, schaufeln	shovel, to shovel
die Schaukel, schaukeln	swing, to swing
der Schaum, schäumen	foam, to foam
das Schauspiel, der Schauspieler	drama/play, actor
der Scheck	check
scheckig	dappled
der Scheffel	bushel
die Scheibe	slice/disk
scheiben = schieben	to shove/to bowl = to push
die Scheide : scheiden, schied, geschieden	borderline : to separate, separated, separated
der Schein, scheinen, schien, geschienen	appearance/shine, to appear/to shine, appeared/shone, appeared/shone
scheinbar	apparently
scheinheilig	sanctimonious
das Scheit, der Scheiterhaufen	piece of wood, stake/pyre
der Scheitel, scheiteln	part, to part (of hair)
scheitern	to fail
der Schellack	shellac
die Schelle, schellen	bell, to ring the bell
der Schelm, schelmisch	imp, impish
schelten, schalt, gescholten, du schiltst, er schilt	to scold, scolded, scolded, you scold, he scolds
der Schemel	footstool
der Schenk, die Schenke	innkeeper, tavern
der Schenkel	thigh
schenken, das Geschenk	to give, gift
der Scherben	shard
die Schere, scheren, scherte oder schor, geschert oder geschoren	pair of scissors, to shear, sheared, sheared
die Schererei	trouble/hassle
der Scherz, scherzen, du scherzt, scherzweise	joke, to joke, you joke, as a joke
die Scheu, scheu, scheuen	shyness, shy, to shy away from
die Scheuche, scheuchen	scarecrow, to shoo
die Scheuer	barn
scheuern = reinigen	to scrub = to clean
die Scheune	barn
das Scheusal	monster
scheußlich	monstrous
die Schicht, Schichtarbeit	shift, shift work
die Schichte, schichten	layer, to layer
der Schick	chic/elegance
schicken, es schickt sich	to be fitting, it is fitting
schicklich	fitting
das Schicksal	destiny
schieben, schob, geschoben	to push, pushed, pushed
der Schieber	pusher/slider
der Schiedsrichter	referee
schief = geneigt	crooked = slanting
der Schiefer	slate
schielen	to be cross-eyed
das Schienbein	shin
die Schiene	track
schier = beinahe	sheer = almost
schießen, schoß, geschossen, du schießt, Schießstätte	to shoot, shot, shot, you shoot, shooting range
das Schiff, schiffen, der Schiffer, schiffbar	ship, to ship, shipper, navigable
die Schiffahrt, Schiff-fahrt	shipping
der Schild : Waffe	shield : weapon
das Schild : Firmenschild	nameplate = company's nameplate
schildern, die Schilderung	to describe, description
das Schildpatt	tortoiseshell
die Schildwache	sentinel
das Schilf	reed
schillern, schillernd	to glitter, opalescent
der Schilling	shilling
der Schimmel	mildew/white horse
der Schimmer, schimmern	shimmer, to shimmer
schimmlig	moldy
der Schimpf, schimpfen	rant, to rant/to insult/to scold
die Schindel	shingle
schinden, geschunden	to maltreat, maltreated
der Schinder, die Schinderei	slave driver, slaving away
der Schinken	ham
der Schirm, schirmen	umbrella, to protect from
schirren, anschirren	to harness a horse, to hitch up
die Schlacht	battle
schlachten, der Schlächter, die Schlächterei	to slaughter, slaughterer, slaughter
die Schlacke	cinders
der Schlaf, schlafen, schlief, geschlafen, du schläfst, schläft	sleep, to sleep, slept, slept, you sleep, sleeps
die Schläfe	temple (of the forehead)
der Schläfer, schläfrig	sleeper, sleepy
schlaff = nicht gespannt	flabby = not taut

der Schlag, Schläge	blow, blows
schlagen, schlug, geschlagen, du schlägst, schlägt	to hit, hit, hit, you hit, hits
der Schlamm	mud
die Schlamperei, schlampig	sloppiness, sloppy
die Schlange	snake
schlängeln	to snake/to wriggle
schlank	slender
schlau, die Schlauheit	clever, cleverness
der Schlauch, Schläuche	hose (sg. & pl.)
schlecht, die Schlechtigkeit	bad, badness
schlecken, die Schleckerei	to lick/to suck on sweets
der Schlegel	leg (of a cow or deer)
schleichen, schlich, geschlichen	to sneak, snuck, snuck
der Schleier	veil
die Schleife	bow
schleifen (Messer), schliff, geschliffen, der Schliff, der Schleifer	to sharpen (knives), sharpened, sharpened, polish, polisher/grinder
schleifen = schleppen; schleifte, geschleift	to drag = to haul; dragged, dragged
der Schleim, schleimig	slime, slimy
schlenkern	to dangle
schleppen, der Schlepper	to drag, tractor
die Schleuder, schleudern	slingshot, to fling
schlichten	to settle (an argument)
schliesen, schloss, geschlossen	to shut, shut, shut
schließen, schloß, geschlossen, du schließt, schließ zu!	to lock, locked, locked, you lock, lock up!
schließlich	finally
der Schliff	grinding/cut (of a diamond)
schlimm	bad
die Schlinge, schlingen, schlang, geschlungen	sling, to sling, slang, slung
der Schlingel	rascal
der Schlitten, Schlitten fahren	sled, to sled
der Schlittschuh, Schlittschuh laufen, der Schlittschuhläufer	ice skate, to ice skate, ice skater
der Schlitz, schlitzen	slit, to slit
das Schloß, des Schlosses, Schlösser	castle, of the castle, castles
die Schlosse (Hagel), Schlossen	large hailstone (hail), large hailstones
der Schlosser, die Schlosserei	locksmith, locksmith's shop
die Schlucht	ravine
schluchzen	to sob
der Schluck, schlucken	sip, to sip/to swallow
der Schlucker = armer Teufel	poor wretch = poor devil
der Schlummer, schlummern	slumber, to slumber
der Schlund, Schlünde	gorge/throat, gorges/throats
der Schlupf, schlüpfen, Schlupfwinkel	slip, to slip, hiding place
schlüpfrig	slippery
schlürfen	to slurp
der Schluß, des Schlusses, Schlüsse	conclusion, of the conclusion, conclusions
der Schlüssel	key
die Schmach	shame/disgrace
schmächtig	slight (of a person)
schmackhaft	tasty
schmal, schmäler oder schmaler	narrow, narrower
das Schmalz, schmalzen, geschmalzen	lard/dripping, cook with dripping, cooked with dripping
der Schmarren	a dessert of hot torn-up pancake
der Schmaus, schmausen	feast, to feast
schmecken	to taste
die Schmeichelei, schmeicheln, der Schmeichler	flattery, to flatter, flatterer
schmeißen, schmiß, geschmissen, du schmeisst	to throw, threw, thrown, you throw
schmelzen = zergehen; schmolz, geschmolzen, es schmilzt	to melt = to dissolve; melted, molten, it melts
schmelzen = flüssigmachen; schmelzte, geschmelzt, die Schmelzerei	to melt = to liquefy; liquefied, liquefied, smeltery
der Schmerz, schmerzen, es schmerzt, schmerzhaft	pain, to be painful, it pains so./it aches, painful
der Schmetterling	butterfly
der Schmied, die Schmiede, schmieden, Schmiedeeisen	blacksmith, blacksmith's shop, to forge, wrought iron
schmiegen, anschmiegen	to snuggle, to nestle
die Schmiere, schmieren	grease, to grease
schmierig	greasy
die Schminke, schminken	makeup, to put on makeup
der Schmirgel, schmirgeln	emery, to sand down
die Schmolle	crumb
der Schmuck, schmücken	jewelry/adornment, to adorn
schmuggeln, der Schmuggler	to smuggle, smuggler
schmunzeln	to smile

der Schmutz, schmutzig	dirt, dirty
der Schnabel, Schnäbel	beak (sg. & pl.)
schnäbeln	to bill/to bill and coo
das Schnaderhüpfel	Alpine version of rap battles
die Schnalle, schnallen	buckle, to buckle
schnalzen	to click one's tongue/to snap one's fingers
schnappen	to snatch
der Schnaps, Schnäpse	schnapps (sg. & pl.)
schnapsen	to booze
schnarchen	to snore
schnarren	to whirr/to buzz
schnattern	to chatter
schnaufen	to pant
die Schnauze	snout
die Schnecke	snail
der Schnee, der Schneeball	snow, snowball
die Schneewehe	snowdrift
Schneid haben	to have guts
die Schneide, schneiden, schnitt, geschnitten, der Schnitt	cutting edge, to cut, cut, cut, cut
der Schneider, schneidern	tailor, to tailor
schneidig	dashing
schneien, schneite, geschneit	to snow, snowed, snowed
schnell, die Schnelligkeit	quick, quickness
schnellen	to dart
die Schnepfe	snipe/woodcock
schneuzen, du schneuzt	to blow one's nose, you blow your nose
der Schnitt	cut
die Schnitte	slice
der Schnitter	reaper
der Schnittlauch	chives
das Schnitzel	schnitzel
schnitzeln	to chop finely
schnitzen, der Schnitzer, Holzschnitzerei	to carve, wood carver, wood carving
der Schnörkel	curlicue
schnorren, der Schnorrer	to mooch, moocher
schnüffeln	to snuffle/to snoop
der Schnupfen, schnupfen	cold, to have a cold
schnuppern	to sniff
die Schnur, Schnüre	string (sg. & pl.)
schnüren	to lace (up)
der Schnurrbart, -bärte	mustache (sg. & pl.)
schnurren	to purr
der Schober, schöbern	rick, to rick
das Schock	sixty
die Schokolade	chocolate
die Scholle	clod (of earth)
schon, wenn schon	already, if it is so
schön, die Schönheit, schöntun	beautiful, beauty, to ingratiate
schonen, die Schonung	to treat with care, rest/good care
die Schonzeit	closed season
der Schopf, Schöpfe	shock of hair/tuft, shocks of hair/tufts
schöpfen, der Schöpfer, die Schöpfung	to create, creator, creation
der Schöps, das Schöpserne	mutton, mutton
der Schorf	scab
der Schornstein	chimney
der Schoß, des Schosses, Schöße	lap, of the lap, laps
der Schößling	sapling
die Schote	pod
der Schotter, schottern	gravel, to gravel
schraffieren	to crosshatch
schräg, die Schräge	slanting, slant
der Schragen	trestle
die Schramme	scratch
der Schrank, Schränke	closet, closets
die Schranke	gate/barrier
die Schraube, schrauben	screw, to screw
der Schraubstock	bench vise
der Schreck, sich schrecken, erschrecken, erschrak, erschrocken, du erschrickst; jemanden schrecken, schreckte, geschreckt	fright, to be frightened, to frighten, frightened, frightened, you are frightened; to frighten so., frightened so., frightened so.
schrecklich	frightful/dreadful
der Schrei, schreien, schrie, geschrien	scream, to scream, screamed, screamed
schreiben, schrieb, geschrieben, das Schrei-ben, der Schreiber, Schreibzeug	to write, wrote, written, writing, writer, writing utensils
schreiten, schritt, geschritten, der Schritt	to stride, strode, strode, footsteps/pace
die Schrift, schriftlich, Schriftführer, Schriftsteller	writing, in writing, minute taker, author
der Schritt, schrittweise	step, step by step
schroff	brusque
schröpfen	to fleece so.
das Schrot u. der Schrot	pellet

schrumpfen	to shrink
der Schub, Schübe	shove (sg. & pl.)
der Schubkarren	wheelbarrow
die Schublade	drawer
schüchtern	shy
der Schuft, schuftig	villain, villainous
schuften	to slog away
der Schuh, Schuhmacher, Schuhplattler	shoe, shoemaker, Bavarian shoe-slapping dance performed by men
die Schuld, schuld sein, du bist Schuld	fault, to be at fault, it's your fault
schulden = schuldig sein	to owe = to be in debt
die Schuldigkeit	indebtedness
die Schule	school
der Schüler, die Schülerin, -innen	pupil, pupil (female), pupils (female)
die Schulter, schultern	shoulder, to shoulder
der Schund, schundig	trash, trashy
der Schupf, schupfen = werfen	shove, to shove = to push
der Schupfen (Hütte)	shed (shelter)
die Schuppe, schuppig	scale, scaly
schüren, der Schürhaken	to poke, poker
der Schurz, die Schürze	mantle, apron
der Schuß, des Schusses, Schüsse	shot, of the shot, shots
die Schüssel	bowl
schusseln, schusslig	to bungle, scatterbrained
der Schuster, schustern	cobbler, to cobble
der Schutt	rubble
schütteln	to shake
schütten	to pour
schütter	sparse/thin (as in hair)
der Schutz, schützen, schützte, geschützt, du schützt	protection, to protect, protected, protected, you protect
der Schütze (Jäger)	shooter (hunter)
schwach, schwächer, am schwächsten	weak, weaker, the weakest
die Schwäche, schwächlich, der Schwächling	weakness, weakly, weakling
der Schwager, die Schwägerin, -innen	brother-in-law, sister-in-law, sisters-in-law
die Schwaig = Alm	alpine dairy farm = alp
die Schwalbe	swallow
der Schwamm, Schwämme, schwammig	sponge, sponges, spongy
schwanken, die Schwankung	to fluctuate, fluctuation
der Schwanz, Schwänze	tail (sg. & pl.)
schwänzen, der Schwänzer	to play hooky, truant
schwären = eitern	to fester = to suppurate
der Schwarm, Schwärme	swarm (sg. & pl.)
schwärmen, der Schwärmer	to enthuse, enthusiast
die Schwarte	skin/hide
schwarz, schwärzer, die Schwärze, schwärzen, schwärzlich	black, blacker, blackness, to blacken, blackish
schwätzen, der Schwätzer	to chatter, chatterbox
schweben	to float
Schweden, schwedisch	Sweden, Swedish
der Schwefel, schwefeln	sulfur, to sulfurate
der Schweif	tail (of a horse or a comet)
schweigen, schwieg, geschwiegen, schweig!	to be silent, was silent, has been silent, be quiet!
schweigsam	discreet/taciturn
das Schwein, der Schweinebraten, das Schweinerne	pig, pork roast, pork
die Schweinerei	dirty trick
der Schweiß, schweißen	sweat, to weld
die Schweiz, der Schweizer, schweizerisch	Switzerland, the Swiss, Swiss
die Schwelle	threshold
schwellen, schwoll, geschwollen, es schwillt, die Schwellung	to swell, swelled, swollen, it swells, swelling
schwemmen	to wash out
der Schwengel	clapper/handle (of a hand pump)
schwenken, die Schwenkung	to pivot, pivoting/swiveling
schwer, die Schwere	heavy, heaviness
schwerfällig	ponderous
die Schwerkraft	gravity
schwerlich	hardly
das Schwert	sword
die Schwester	sister
die Schwiele, schwielig	callus, callused
schwierig, die Schwierigkeit	difficult, difficulty
schwimmen, schwamm, geschwommen, der Schwimmer	to swim, swam, swum, swimmer
der Schwindel, schwindeln	swindle, to swindle
schwinden, schwand, geschwunden	to dwindle, dwindled, dwindled
der Schwindler	swindler
schwindlig	dizzy
die Schwindsucht, schwindsüchtig	consumption, consumptive
schwingen, schwang, geschwungen, die Schwingung	to swing, swinged, swinged, vibration

schwirren	to whirr
schwitzen, schwitzte, geschwitzt, du schwitzt	to sweat, sweated, sweated, you sweat
schwören, schwor, geschworen	to swear, swore, sworn
schwül, die Schwüle	muggy, mugginess
der Schwung, Schwünge	swing (sg. & pl.)
der Schwur, Schwüre	oath, oaths
das Sech (Pflug)	colter (plow)
sechs, die Sechs = der Sechser, das Sechste, sechste, das Sechstel	six, the six = the number six, the sixth, sixth, a sixth
sechzehn, sechzig	sixteen, sixty
seckant, die Seckatur	bothersome, bother
seckieren = necken, quälen	to pester = to tease, to torment
der See = Landsee	lake = pond
die See = das Meer	sea = ocean
die Seele	soul
das Segel, segeln	sail, to sail
der Segen, segnen	blessing, to bless
sehen, sah, gesehen, ich sehe, du siehst, er sieht, sieh!	to see, saw, seen, I see, you see, he sees, see!
die Sehenswürdigkeit	sight (as in sightseeing)
die Sehne, sehnig	tendon, sinewy
sehnen, die Sehnsucht	to long, longing
sehr	very
seicht	shallow
seid, ihr seid (von sein)	are, you are (from to be)
die Seide, seiden = aus Seide	silk, silken = of silk
das Seidel (Bier)	stein (beer mug)
die Seife, einseifen	soap, to soap
seihen, seihte, geseiht, der Seiher	to sieve, sieved, sieved, colander
das Seil, der Seiler	rope, ropemaker
sein, war, gewesen, bin, bist, ist, sind, seid, sind, ich wäre, sei brav! seid brav!	to be, was, been, am, are, is, are, are, are, I would be, be good! be good! (pl.)
sein, seine	his, his
seinerzeit	at that time
seinetwegen	for his sake
seinig, seinige, das Seinige	his (inflected)
seit der Zeit, seit gestern usw.	since the time, since yesterday etc.
seitdem, seither	since then, since that time
die Seite, das Ding hat zwei Seiten, Buchseite	side/page, the thing has two sides, book page
seitlich, seitwärts	at the side, sideways
der Sekretär	writing desk/secretary
die Sekunde	second
selber, selbst	self, by oneself
selbständig	independent/autonomous
der Selbstlaut	vowel
selbstverständlich	self-evident
selchen, der Selcher, die Selcherei, Geselchtes	to smoke (meat), butcher/smoker, smokehouse, smoked meat
selig, die Seligkeit	blessed, blessedness
der Sellerie	celery
selten, die Seltenheit	rare, rarity
seltsam	strange
das Semester	semester
die Semmel	bread roll
senden, sandte oder sendete, gesandt oder gesendet, die Sendung	to send, sent, sent, shipment
der Senf	mustard
sengen = brennen; sengte	to singe = to burn; singed
senken : hinunterlassen; senkte, gesenkt	to lower = to let down; lowered, lowered
die Senkgrube	cesspool
senkrecht	vertical
der Senn, der Senne	alpine shepherd (sg. & pl.)
die Sennerin, -innen	alpine shepherdess (sg. & pl.)
die Sense	scythe
separat	separate
Sepp = Josef	Sepp = Joseph
der September	September
die Serpentine	hairpin bend/winding road
servieren	to serve
die Serviette	napkin
servus!	hello!
der Sessel	armchair
setzen, setzte, gesetzt, du setzst, setz dich! der Setzer	to sit, sat, sat, you sit, sit down!, typesetter
die Seuche	epidemic
seufzen, der Seufzer	to sigh, sigh
die Sichel, sicheln	sickle, to cut with a sickle
sicher, die Sicherheit, die Sicherung	secure, security/safety, safety devices/fuse
die Sicht, sichtbar	view/sight, visible
sickern, versickern	to seep/to trickle, to seep away/to trickle away
sie, in der Anrede groß zu schreiben : gehen Sie!	you, to be capitalized : you go!
das Sieb, sieben	sieve, to sieve

sieben, die Sieben = der Siebener; der siebente Tag	seven, the seven = the number seven; the seventh day
siebzehn, siebzig	seventeen, seventy
siedeln = ansiedeln	to settle = to take up residence
sieden, sott, gesotten, der Siedepunkt	to simmer, simmered, simmered, boiling point
der Sieg, siegen, der Sieger	victory, to win, winner
das Siegel, siegeln, der Siegellack	seal, to seal, sealing wax
Siegfried	Siegfried
das Signal	signal
die Silbe, einsilbig	syllable, monosyllabic
das Silber, silbern	silver, silver
Silvester, der Silvesterabend	New Year's, New Year's Eve
sind, wir sind (von sein)	are, we are (from to be)
singen (Lied), sang, gesungen	to sing (song), sang, sung
sinken = fallen; sank, gesunken	to sink = to fall; sank, sunk/sunken
der Sinn, sinnlos	meaning, meaningless
der Siphon	siphon
der Sirup	syrup
die Sitte	custom/tradition
der Sitz, sitzen, saß, gesessen, du sitzt, sitz!	seat, to sit, sat, sat, you sit, sit!
die Sitzung	session/meeting
die Skala, Skalen	scale (sg. & pl.)
der Skandal	scandal
das Skelett	skeleton
der Ski, Skier	ski, skis
die Skizze, skizzieren	sketch, to sketch
der Sklave, sklavisch	slave, slavish
der Slawe, slawisch	the Slav, Slavic
so, so groß, so sehr, sofort	so, so big, so much, at once
die Socke	sock
der Sockel (Säule)	plinth (column)
die Soda	soda
das Sofa	sofa
sofort	at once
sogar	even
sogenannt	so-called
die Sohle = Fußsohle; sohlen	sole = sole of the foot; to sole
der Sohn, Söhne	son (sg. & pl.)
solcher, solche, solches	such (inflected)
der Soldat	soldier
die Sole = Salzwasser	brine = saltwater
solid	solid
sollen, sollte, du sollst	should, should have, you should
der Sommer	summer
die Sommerfrische, der Sommerfrischler	summer vacation, summer vacationist
sonderbar	strange
sondern	instead/but rather
die Sonne, sich sonnen, sonnig, Sonnenaufgang	sun, to sunbathe, sunny, sunrise
der Sonntag, sonntags	Sunday, on Sundays
sonst, sonstig	else, other
Sophie	Sophie
die Sorge, sorgen	care/worry, to care/to worry
die Sorgfalt, sorgfältig	care, careful
die Sorte	kind
sortieren	to sort
sowohl	as well as
der Sozialdemokrat, sozial-demokratisch, der Sozialist, sozialistisch	social democrat, social democratic, socialist, socialistic
der Spagat	splits
das Spalier	trellis
der Spalt, die Spalte	crack, cleft
spalten, gespalten	to split, split
der Span, Späne	chip (sg. & pl.)
das Spanferkel	suckling pig
die Spange	barrette
Spanien, spanisch	Spain, Spanish
spannen, spannend, die Spannung	to tighten, exciting, tension
spännig, einspännig, zweispännig, der Einspänner usw.	drawn by horse, drawn by one horse, drawn by two horses, one-horse carriage etc.
sparen, die Sparkasse	to save, savings bank
sparsam, die Sparsamkeit	thrifty, thriftiness
der Spaß, Späße, spaßen, spaßig	joke, jokes, to joke, comical
spät, später, spätestens	late, later, by the latest
der Spaten	spade
der Spatz, das Spätzlein	sparrow, little sparrow
spazieren, der Spaziergang	to stroll, stroll
der Specht	woodpecker
der Speck, speckig	bacon, fatty
der Spediteur	hauler
der Speer	spear
die Speiche (Rad)	spoke (wheel)
der Speichel (Mund)	saliva (mouth)
der Speicher, aufspeichern	storehouse/attic, to store up

speien, spie, gespien	to spit, spit, spit
die Speis = Speisekammer	larder = pantry
die Speise, speisen	meal, to have a meal
das Spektakel	spectacle
spekulieren	to speculate
die Spennadel	straight pin
die Spende, spenden, spendieren	gift, to give, to provide
spendeln = zustecken	to pin = to pin together
spendieren	to provide/to treat (so. to sth.)
der Spengler	plumber
sperren, die Sperre	to block off, barrier
die Spesen	expenses
die Spezerei	spice/spice store
der Spezialist, die Spezialität	specialist, specialty
speziell	special/particular
spezifisches Gewicht	specific weight
spicken (Speck)	to lard (bacon)
der Spiegel, spiegeln	mirror, to mirror
das Spiel, spielen	play/game, to play
die Spielerei	child's play
der Spieß, spießen, aufspießen	skewer, to skewer, to spear
der Spinat	spinach
die Spindel	spindle
die Spinne, das Spinnweb	spider, spiderweb
spinnen, spann, gesponnen, die Spinnerei	to spin, spun, spun, spinning mill
der Spion, spionieren	spy, to spy
die Spirale, Spiralfeder	spiral, spiral spring
der Spiritus, Spirituosen	spirit, spirits (as in liquor)
das Spital, Spitäler	hospital (sg. & pl.)
der Spitz = die Spitze; spitz = spitzig; spitzen	peak = top; pointed = pointy; to sharpen/to prick up
der Spitzel	informer
der Spitzhund	spitz
der Splitter, splittern	splinter, to splinter
die Spore	spore
der Sporn, spornen	spur, to spur
der Sport, der Sportmann	sport, sportsman
der Spott, spotten, spöttisch	mockery, to mock, mocking
die Sprache, Sprachlehre	language, grammar
sprechen, sprach, gesprochen, ich spreche, du sprichst, spricht, sprich!	to speak, spoke, spoken, I speak, you speak, speaks, speak!
die Spreize, spreizen, du spreizt	strut/support, spread, you spread
sprengen, die Sprengung	to detonate, explosion
sprenkeln, gesprenkelt	to sprinkle, sprinkled
die Spreu	chaff
das Sprichwort	proverb
die Sprieße, das Sprießel	strut, brace
sprießen, sproß, gesprossen	to sprout, sprouted, sprouted
springen, sprang, gesprungen, der Springer	to jump, jumped, jumped, jumper
die Spritze, spritzen, spritzte	syringe, to inject, injected
spröde, spröd	brittle, stand-offish
der Sproß, Sprosse	shoot/scion, offspring/rung
der Sprößling	offspring
die Sprosse = Leitersprosse	step = rung of a ladder
sprossen, sproßte, gesprosst	to sprout, sprouted, sprouted
der Spruch, Sprüche	saying, proverbs
der Sprudel, sprudeln, der Sprudler	sparkling mineral water, to bubble, blender
sprühen, sprühte, gesprüht	to spray, sprayed, sprayed
der Sprung, Sprünge	jump/leap, jumps/leaps
spucken, Spucknapf	to spit, spittoon
die Spule, spulen	spool, to spool
spülen, abspülen	to wash up, to wash off
der Spund, Spünde	plug (sg. & pl.)
die Spur	trace
spüren	to sense sth./to feel sth.
der Staat, staatlich	state, state
der Stab, Stäbe, das Stäbchen	rod, rods, small rod
der Stachel	thorn
der Stadel	barn
die Stadt, Städte, städtisch, Stadttor	town, towns, urban, city gate
die Staffel	relay
die Staffelei	easel
staffieren, ausstaffieren	to pad, to equip sth. with sth.
der Stahl (Eisen), stählern	steel (iron), steel
der Stall : Viehstall; Ställe	stable : cattle stable; stables
der Stamm, Stämme	trunk, trunks (of a tree)
stammeln	to stammer
stammen = abstammen	to stem = to descend from
stampfen, die Stampfe	to ram (down), wooden rammer
der Stand, Stände, imstand sein, er ist imstand	stand, stands/state (of), states (of), to be capable of, he is capable of
der Ständer	rack
standhaft	steadfast

der Satan (Satan)

die Stange	bar
das Stanniol	tinfoil
die Stanze, stanzen	die cutter, to die-cut
stapeln, aufstapeln	to pile, to pile up
stapfen	to trudge
der Star	starling
stark, stärker, am stärksten	strong, stronger, strongest
die Stärke, stärken, die Stärkung	strength, to strengthen, refreshment
starr, erstarren	rigid, to freeze (figurative)
der Start, starten	start, to start
stätig	stubborn/mulish (of a horse)
die Station	station
das Stativ	tripod
statt = anstatt	instead of = in the place of
die Stätte = Platz; Brandstätte	place = site; scene of fire
die Statue	statue
die Statur	figure
der Staub, stauben, staubig	dust, to dust, dusty
die Staude	shrub
stauen, die Stauung	to congest, congestion
staunen	to marvel
stechen, stach, gestochen, ich steche, du stichst, sticht, stich! der Stich	to sting, stung, stung, I sting, you sting, stings, sting! sting
stecken, steckte, gesteckt	to stick, stuck, stuck
der Stecken	stick
die Stecknadel	pin
der Steg	pier
steh(e)n, stand, gestanden, du stehst, steht, steh!	to stand, stood, stood, you stand, stands, stand!
stehlen (Dieb), stahl, gestohlen, ich stehle, du stiehlst, stiehlt	to steal (thief), stole, stolen, I steal, you steal, steals
die Steiermark	Styria
steif, die Steifheit	stiff, stiffness
steifen, sich auf etwas steifen	to stiffen, to be (become) set on sth.
der Steig	steep and narrow path
steigen, stieg, gestiegen, die Steigung	to climb, climbed, climbed, incline
der Steiger	foreman of miners/riser
steil	steep
der Stein, steinern, steinhart	stone, stone, as hard as stone
der Steinmetz	stonemason
der Steirer, steirisch	the Styrian, Styrian

die Stelle, stellen (hinstellen), stellte, gestellt, stellenweise	place, to place (to set down), placed, placed, in places
die Stellung	position
der Stellvertreter	substitute
der Stellwagen	horse-drawn vehicle
die Stelze	stilt
stemmen, das Stemmeisen	to heave, crowbar
der Stempel, stempeln	stamp, to stamp
der Stengel	stalk
die Stenographie, stenographieren	stenography, to take shorthand
Stephan, Stephanie	Stephen, Stephanie
die Steppe	steppe/prairie (in North America)
steppen, die Steppdecke	to quilt, quilt
sterben, starb, gestorben, ich sterbe, du stirbst, sterblich	to die, died, died, I die, you die, mortal
der Stern	star
der Sterz	rump
die Steuer (Geldbetrag)	tax (money)
das Steuer (am Schiff), steuern	helm (in a boat), to steer
der Stich, sticheln	stab, to taunt
sticken, die Stickerei	to embroider, embroidery
der Stickstoff	nitrogen
der Stiefel	boot
das Stiefkind, Stiefmutter usw.	stepchild, stepmother etc.
die Stiege	stairs (steep and narrow)
der Stieglitz	goldfinch
der Stiel = Stengel, Griff	shaft = stalk, handle
der Stier	bull
stieren, anstieren	to glare, to stare at
der Stift, Bleistift	pen, pencil
das Stift = Kloster	convent = cloister
stiften, die Stiftung	to donate, donation
der Stil : Baustil	style : building style
still : ruhig; die Stille	still : quiet; silence
stillen	to nurse
die Stimme	voice
stimmen	to tune/to vote
die Stimmung	mood/atmosphere
stinken, stank, gestunken, stinkig, der Gestank	to stink, stank, stunk, stinky, stink
die Stirne	forehead
stöbern	to rummage
der Stocher, stochern	toothpick/poker, to pick

der Stock, Stöcke	stick, (sg. & pl.)
stocken	to halt/to thicken
stockfinster	pitch-black
der Stoßzahn	tusk
der Stoff	fabric
stöhnen	to moan
die Stola	stole
der Stollen	stollen
stolpern	to stumble
der Stolz, stolz	pride, proud
stopfen	to stuff/to mend
der Stoppel, zustoppeln	cork, to stopple
die Stoppel, Stoppelfeld	stubble, stubble field
der Stöpsel, stöpseln	plug, to plug
der Storch, Störche	stork (sg. & pl.)
stören, die Störung	to interrupt, interruption
störrisch	stubborn
der Stoß, Stöße, stoßen, stieß, gestoßen, ich stoße, du stößt	push, pushes, to push, pushed, pushed, I push, you push
der Stößel	pestle
stottern, der Stotterer	to stutter, stutterer
die Strafe, strafen	punishment, to punish
straff gespannt	tightly stretched
sträflich, der Sträfling	criminal, prisoner
der Strahl, strahlen	ray, radiate
der Strähn, strähnen	strand/streak/skein, to form sth. from strands/to make streaks on/to wind into skeins
stramm	tight
strampeln	to kick
der Strand	beach
der Strang, Stränge, strängen = anbinden	rope, ropes, to rope = to tie up
die Strapaze, strapazieren	strain, to be a strain on
die Straße	street
sträuben, sich sträuben	to refuse/to bristle
der Strauch, Sträucher	shrub (sg. & pl.)
der Strauchen = Schnupfen	cold = head cold
der Strauß, Sträuße	bouquet (sg. & pl.)
streben, der Streber	to strive, teacher's pet
die Strecke	distance/stretch
strecken, streckte, gestreckt	to extend, extended, extended
der Streich	prank
streicheln	to pet
streichen, strich, gestrichen	to paint, painted, painted
der Streifen	band/strip
streifen, herumstreifen	to roam, to roam around
der Streik, streiken	strike, to strike
der Streit, streiten, stritt, gestritten	argument/quarrel, to argue/to quarrel, argued/quarreled, argued/quarreled
streng, die Strenge	strict, srictness
die Streu, streuen	litter, to scatter
der Strich, stricheln	stroke, to dot/line/to draw in a series of little strokes
der Strick	rope
stricken, die Strickerei	to knit, knitting
der Striegel, striegeln	currycomb, to currycomb/to brush
der Striezel	braided bread
das Stroh, Strohhut	straw, straw hat
der Strolch, strolchen	scoundrel, to roam
der Strom, Ströme, stromabwärts	stream, streams, downstream
strömen, die Strömung	to stream, current
die Strophe	stanza/verse
strotzen	to brim (over with)
der Strudel, strudeln	whirlpool, to whirl
der Strumpf, Strümpfe	stocking (sg. & pl.)
der Strunk, Strünke	stalk/stump, stalks/stumps
die Strupfe, strupfen	slip-knot, to slip off
struppig	shaggy
die Stube, das Stübchen	parlor, cozy little room
der Stüber	flick/reprimand
der Stuck, die Stukkatur	stucco, stucco work
das Stück, stückeln	piece, to cut sth. into pieces
der Student, studieren	student, to study
die Stufe	step
der Stuhl, Stühle	chair (sg. & pl.)
die Stukkatur	stucco work
stülpen	to put over/to slip over
stumm	mute
der Stummel	stub
der Stümper, stümpern	bungler, to blunder
der Stumpf, Stümpfe, stumpf	stump, stumps, blunt/dull
der Stumpfsinn	dullness
die Stunde, stundenlang, stündlich	hour, for hours, hourly
stupfen	to nudge
der Sturm, Stürme, stürmen, stürmisch	storm, storms, to storm, stormy
der Sturz, Stürze, stürzen	fall, falls, to fall

die Stute	mare
die Stütze, stützen, stützte	support, to support, supported
stutzen, stutzte, gestutzt	to trim/to become suspicious, trimmed/became suspicious, trimmed/became suspicious
stutzig	to be taken aback
subtrahieren, die Subtraktion	to subtract, subtraction
suchen, auf der Suche	to search, to go and search
die Sucht, ... süchtig	addiction, ... addicted
der Sud (von sieden)	broth (from to simmer)
der Süden, im Süden, südlich, Südost, südöstlich, Südwest, südwestlich, Südpol	South, in the South, southern, Southeast, southeast, Southwest, southwest, South Pole
der Suff	boozing
der Sultan	sultan
die Sulz, Sulze	aspic, jellied meat
die Summe, summieren	sum, to sum
summen	to hum
der Sumpf, Sümpfe, sumpfig	swamp, swamps, swampy
die Sünde, der Sünder, sündigen	sin, sinner, to sin
die Suppe	soup
surren	to buzz
süß, süßer, am süßesten, die Süßigkeit, süßlich	sweet, sweeter, sweetest, sweets, sweetish
der Sweater = Leibchen	sweater = undershirt
symmetrisch, die Symmetrie	symmetrical, symmetry
sympathisch	likeable
die Szene	scene

T

der Tabak	tobacco
die Tabelle	table (as in tabulation)
das Tabernakel	tabernacle
der Tadel, tadeln	reprimand, to reprimand
tadellos	flawless
die Tafel, täfeln	blackboard, to panel
der Tag, Tage, täglich	day, days, daily
die Taille	waist
der Takt, taktieren	time/measure, to beat time
das Tal, Täler	valley (sg. & pl.)
der Taler	taler
das Talent	talent
der Talg	tallow/suet

tandeln, der Tandler	to dawdle, dawdler
die Tanne	fir tree
die Tante	aunt
der Tanz, Tänze, tanzen, du tanzt	dance, dances, to dance, you dance
die Tapete, tapezieren	wallpaper, to wallpaper
tapfer, die Tapferkeit	brave, bravery
tappen, täppisch	to grope (one's way), awkward
die Tara	tare
tarieren	to tare
der Tarif	tariff
die Tasche, Taschentuch	bag, handkerchief
die Tasse	cup
die Taste, der Taster	key, button/switch
tasten	to feel/to touch
die Tat, der Täter	act/deed, offender
tätig, die Tätigkeit	active, activity
die Tatsache, tatsächlich	fact, actually
die Tatze	paw
das Tau = Seil	rope = cord
der Tau, tauen, es taut	dew, to thaw, it thaws
taub, der Taube, taubstumm	deaf, deaf person, deaf-mute
die Taube, der Tauber, das Täubchen	pigeon, cock pigeon, dove
tauchen, der Taucher	to dive, diver
tauen, es taut	to thaw, it thaws
die Taufe, taufen, Taufpate, Taufname, der Täufling	baptism, to baptize, godfather/godparent, baptismal name, child to be baptized
taugen, tauglich	to be suitable for, suitable
taumeln	to reel/to stagger
der Tausch, tauschen	exchange, to exchange
täuschen, die Täuschung	to deceive, deception
tausend, viele Tausende, der Tausender, tausendmal, das Tausendstel, tausendste	thousand, many thousands, the number thousand, a thousand times, thousandth, the thousandth
die Taxe, der Taxameter	fee/taxi, taximeter
die Technik, der Techniker	technology, technician
der Tee	tea
der Teer	tar
der Teich	pond
der Teig, teigig	dough, doughy
der Teil, teilen, die Teilung	part, to divide, division
die Teilnahme	participation
teilnehmen, ich nehme teil, der Teilnehmer	to participate, I participate, participant

teils, größtenteils	in part, mainly
teilweise	partial
das Telegramm, der Telegraph, telegraphieren, telegraphisch	telegram, telegraph, to telegraph, telegraphic
das Telephon, telephonieren, telephonisch	telephone, to telephone, telephonic/by phone
der Teller	plate
der Tempel	temple
die Temperatur	temperature
das Tempo	tempo
der Tender	tender
die Tenne	threshing floor
der Teppich	carpet
der Termin	appointment
die Terrasse	terrace
die Terz	third (music)
das Testament	testament
teuer, die Teuerung	expensive, increase in prices
der Teufel, teuflisch	devil, devilish
der Text	text
die Textilindustrie	textile industry
des Theater	theater
Theodor	Theodore
die Theorie, theoretisch	theory, theoretical
Therese, Theresia	Teresa, Theresa
das Thermometer	thermometer
Thomas	Thomas
der Thron	throne
ticken	to tick
tief, die Tiefe	deep, depth
der Tiegel	small container
das Tier, tierisch	animal, animalistic
der Tiger	tiger
tilgen, vertilgen	to delete sth., to exterminate/to annul/to eradicate
die Tinte, tintig	ink, inky
Tirol, tirolerisch	the Tyrol, Tyrolean
der Tisch	table
der Tischler, die Tischlerei, tischlern	carpenter, carpentry, to carpenter
der Titel	title
toben	to romp
Tobias	Tobias
die Tochter, Töchter	daughter, daughters
der Tod, todkrank, tödlich; aber: tot	death, critically ill, deadly; but: dead
toll, die Tollwut	mad/great, rabies
der Ton = Töpferton; tönern = aus Ton	clay = pottery clay; earthen/clay = made of clay
der Ton : Klang; Töne, tönen = klingen	tone : sound; tones, to sound = to ring
Toni = Anton	Tony = Anthony
die Tonne	ton/tub
der Topf, Töpfe	pot (sg. & pl.)
der Topfen	curd
der Töpfer, töpfern	potter, to make pottery
das Tor	gate
der Torf, das Torfmoor	peat, peat bog
torkeln	to stagger
die Torte	torte
tot, töten, totschlagen, der Tote; aber: der Tod	dead, to kill, to strike dead, dead body; but: death
total	total
die Tour, der Tourist	tour, tourist
der Trab, traben	trot, to trot
die Tracht	traditional costume
trachten	to strive to
trächtig	pregnant (of an animal)
die Trafik, die Trafikantin, -innen	tobacconist's shop, tobacconist (female), tobacconists (female)
träg, die Trägheit	lethargic/idle, lethargy/idleness
tragen, trug, getragen, du trägst, trägt, der Träger	to carry, carried, carried, you carry, carries, carrier
tragisch	tragic
traktieren	to bully so.
der Trampel, trampeln	clumsy oaf, to tramp
die Tramway = Straßenbahn	tram = streetcar
die Träne, tränen	tear, to tear (as in weep)
der Trank, Tränke	drink, drinking trough
die Tränke, tränken	drinking trough, to water/to saturate
die Transmission	transmission
der Transport, transportieren	transport, to transport
das Trapez	trapeze
der Tratsch, tratschen	gossip, to gossip
die Traube	grape
trauen	to wed so./to trust so./to dare sth.
die Trauer, trauern	mourning, to mourn
der Traum, träumen	dream, to dream
traurig, die Traurigkeit	sad, sadness
die Trauung	wedding
die Travestie	travesty

treffen, traf, getroffen, ich treffe, du triffst, trifft	to meet, met, met, I meet, you meet, meets
der Treffer	hit
treiben, trieb, getrieben, der Treiber, der Trieb	to drive, drive, driven, herder, drive/instinct
trennen, die Trennung	to separate, separation
die Treppe	stairs
treten, trat, getreten, ich trete, du trittst, er tritt, der Tritt	to kick, kicked, kicked, I kick, you kick, he kicks, kick
treu, die Treue, treulos	loyal, loyalty, disloyal
Tribüne	platform/bleachers
der Trichter, eintrichtern	funnel, to drum sth. into so.
der Trieb	drive/instinct
triefen, troff, getroffen	to be sopping wet, was sopping wet, had been sopping wet
das Trikot	leotard/jersey
der Triller, trillern	trill, to trill
trinken, trank, getrunken, der Trank, der Trinker	to drink, drank, drunk, drink, drinker
das Trinkgeld	tip (as in gratuity)
trippeln	to trip (as in to patter)
der Tritt	kick/step/footfall
trocken, die Trockenheit	dry, dryness/drought
trocknen	to dry
trödeln, der Trödler	to dally, slow-poke
der Trog, Tröge	trough, troughs
die Trommel, trommeln	drum, to drum
die Trompete, der Trompeter	trumpet, trumpeter
der Tropfen, tropfen, tröpfeln	drop, to drip, to trickle
der Trost, trösten, trostlos	consolation, to console, bleak
der Trottel	moron
das Trottoir (sprich : Trottuar) = Gehsteig	pavement = sidewalk
trotz : trotzdem	in spite of : nonetheless
der Trotz, trotzen, trotzte, getrotzt, trotzig	defiance, to defy, defied, defied, defiant
trüb, trüben = trüb machen	cloudy/muddy, to cloud = to make cloudy/to muddy = to make muddy
trübselig	melancholy
der Trug, trügen	deceit, to deceive
die Truhe	chest (piece of furniture)
das Trumm, die Trümmer	lump, rubble
der Trunk, betrunken	drink, drunk
der Trupp, die Truppe	squad, troop
der Truthahn, -hähne	turkey (sg. & pl.)
die Truthenne, -hennen	turkey-hen, turkey-hens
der Tscheche, tschechisch	the Czech, Czech
die Tschechoslowakei	Czechoslovakia
tuberkulos, die Tuberkulose	consumptive, tuberculosis
das Tuch, Tücher	cloth (sg. & pl.)
tüchtig, die Tüchtigkeit	efficient, efficiency
tückisch	malicious
tüfteln	to fiddle (about)/to tinker
die Tugend	virtue
tummeln	to romp
der Tümpel	tarn
tun, tat, getan, ich tu, du tust, er tut, tu das nicht!	to do, did, done, I do, you do, he does, don't do that!
tünchen, der Tüncher	to whitewash walls, house painter
tunken	to dip sth. into sth.
der Tunnel	tunnel
der Tupf, tupfen, tüpfeln	dot, to dab, to dot
die Tür, oder die Türe	door
die Turbine	turbine
der Türke, türkisch, die Türkei	the Turk, Turkish, Turkey
der Turm, Türme, auftürmen	tower, towers, to tower
turnen, der Turner	to do gymnastics, gymnast
die Turteltaube	turtle dove
die Tusche (Tinte)	India ink (ink)
tuscheln	to whisper
die Tüte	bag
der Typhus : Krankheit	typhoid : illness

U

das Übel, übel, die Übelkeit	evil/ill, evil/ill, nausea
üben, die Übung	to practice, practice
über, übers = über das	above/over/beyond/about = above the/over the/ beyond the/about the
überall	all over
überdrüssig	weary/tired of sth.
übereinander	on top of each other
der Überfluß, überflüssig	abundance, superfluous
überhaupt	at all
überlegen	superior/to reflect
der Übermut, übermütig	high spirits, high-spirited
überraschen, die Überraschung	to surprise, surprise
die Überschrift	heading
der Überschuß, überschüssig	surplus, surplus

überschwemmen, die Überschwemmung	to flood, flood
die Übersicht, übersichtlich	overview, manageable
übersiedeln, die Übersiedlung	emigrate, emigration
überwinden, -wand, -wunden, die Überwindung	to overcome, overcame, overcome, overcoming/conscious effort
überzeugen, die Überzeugung	to persuade, conviction
übrig	left over/residual
übrigens	by the way
die Übung	practice/exercise
das Ufer	shore
die Uhr, wie viel Uhr ist es?	clock, what time is it?
um; ums = um das	around; around the/for = for the
umarmen	to hug
umeinander	around each other
der Umfang, Umfänge	circumference (sg. & pl.)
der Umgang, Umgänge	social interaction/procession, social interactions/processions (rel.)
umher	around
der Umschlag, Umschläge	envelope (sg. & pl.)
umsonst	free of charge/futile
der Umweg	detour
unangenehm	unpleasant
die Unannehmlichkeit	unpleasantness
die Unart, unartig	mischief, mischievous
unaufhörlich	incessant/perpetual
unausstehlich	intolerable
unbändig	unruly
unbedingt	unconditional/absolutely
unbeholfen	clumsy
und, und so fort	and, and so on
unerhört	outrageous
der Unfall, Unfälle	accident (sg. & pl.)
der Unfug	nonsense/mischief
der Ungar, Ungarn, ungarisch	the Hungarian, Hungary, Hungarian
ungefähr	approximately
ungeheuer, das Ungeheuer	monstrous, monster
das Ungetüm	behemoth
das Ungeziefer	vermin
unglaublich	incredible
die Uniform	uniform
die Universität	university
das Unkraut	weeds

unnötig	unnecessary
der Unrat	refuse/trash
der Unschlitt	tallow
unser, unsere, unserig, unsrig, unsereiner	our, ours, ours, ours, the likes of us/we
der Unsinn, unsinnig	nonsense, nonsensical
unsrig, unsrige, der Unsrige	ours (inflected)
unten	down below
unter, unterm = unter dem; untern = unter den; unters = unter das; unter den; unters = unter das; untere, unterste	below, below the; below the, below the; lower, lowest
unterdes, unterdessen	by then, meanwhile
untereinander	among each other/one under the other
unterhalb	below/underneath
unterhalten, -hielt, die Unterhaltung	to entertain, entertained, entertainment
unternehmen, -nahm, -nommen, -nimmst	to undertake/to venture, undertook/ventured, undertaken/ventured, you undertake/you venture
Unterricht, unterrichten	teaching, to teach
unterscheiden, -schieden	to distinguish/to differ, distinguished/differed
Unterschied	distinction/difference
unterschlächtig	undershot (of a waterwheel)
die Unterschrift	signature
der Unterstand, -stände	shelter (sg. & pl.)
der Untertan	subject (e.g., of a monarch)
unterwegs	on the way
ununterbrochen	continuous
unvermutet	unexpected
unverschämt, die Unverschämtheit	impertinent, impertinence
unversehens	suddenly
unwahr, die Unwahrheit	untrue, untruth
das Unwetter	storm
unwillkürlich	involuntary
unwohl, das Unwohlsein	unwell, indisposition
die Unzahl, unzählig	immense number, countless
uralt	age-old
der Urenkel, Urgroßvater usw.	great-grandchild, great-grandfather etc.
die Urkunde	certificate/deed
der Urlaub	vacation
die Urne	urn
die Ursache	cause/reason
der Ursprung, Ursprünge	origin (sg. & pl.)
ursprünglich	originally

Ursula	Ursula
das Urteil, urteilen	judgment, to judge

V

der Vagabund	vagabond
die Valuta	value/valuta
die Vanille	vanilla
die Vase	vase
das Vaselin	Vaseline
der Vater, Väter, väterlich, das Vaterunser	father, fathers, fatherly, Lord's Prayer
vazieren, vazierend	to move from place to place, moving from place to place
das Veilchen	violet (plant)
die Vene	vein
das Ventil, die Ventilation	valve/vent, ventilation
die Venus	Venus
ver...	inseparable verbal prefix indicating a faulty action or connection
verabreden, die Verabredung	to arrange sth., meeting/appointment
verachten, die Verachtung	to scorn, contempt
die Veranda, Veranden	porch (sg. & pl.)
veranlagt, die Veranlagung	predisposed, predisposition
veranlassen, -lasste, -lasst, die Veranlassung	to arrange for sth., arranged for sth., arranges for sth., reason
veranstalten, die Veranstaltung	to organize, event
verantworten	to take the responsibility for
die Verantwortung	responsibility
der Verband, Verbände	association (sg. & pl.)
verbergen, -barg, -borgen, -birgst	to hide, hid, hidden, you hide
verbessern, die Verbesserung	to improve, improvement
verbieten, -bot, -boten, das Verbot	to forbid, forbade, forbidden, ban
die Verbindung	connection
verbitten = sich etwas verbitten; -bat, -beten, das verbitte ich mir; aber: ich verbiete dir...	to refuse to tolerate, refused to tolerate, refused to tolerate; I refuse to tolerate this; but: I forbid you to...
verblüffen	to perplex
das Verbot	ban
das Verbrechen	crime
verbreiten, die Verbreitung	to spread, spread/distribution
die Verbrennung	burn/burning
der Verdacht, verdächtig	suspicion, suspicious
verdammen, verdammt	to condemn, damned
verdauen, die Verdauung	to digest, digestion
verderben, verdarb, verdorben, ich verberbe, du verdirbst, verdirbt	to spoil, spoiled, spoiled, I spoil, you spoil, spoils
verdienen, der Verdienst = Bezahlung; das Verdienst = ausgezeichnete Leistung	to earn, earnings = payment; merit = outstanding achievement
verdingen, verdungen	to hire so. out, hired so. out
verdorren	to wither
verdrießen, verdroß, verdrossen, verdrießlich	to irk, irked, irked, peevish
der Verdruß	chagrin
verdutzt	puzzled
der Verein, vereinigen	union, to unite
verenden	to perish
verflixt	darned
die Vergangenheit	past
vergebens, vergeblich	in vain, futile
vergelten, -galt, -golten, -giltst, -gilt, die Vergeltung	to avenge, avenged, avenged, you avenge, avenges, revenge
vergessen, vergaß, sie vergaßen, du vergißt, vergiß! vergeßlich	to forget, forgot, they forgot, you forget, forget! forgetful
das Vergißmeinnicht	forget-me-not
vergeuden, die Vergeudung	to squander, squandering
der Vergleich, vergleichen, -glich, -glichen	comparison, to compare, compared, compared
das Vergnügen, vergnügt	amusement/delight, amused/delighted
verhaften	to arrest
das Verhältnis, -nisse	relation(ship) (sg. & pl.)
verhältnismäßig	relatively/commensurate to
verhehlen	to conceal
verheimlichen	to withhold (information)/to keep secret
verhindern	to prevent
das Verhör, verhören	interrogation, to interrogate
verhungern	to starve (to death)
verirren	to stray/to go astray
der Verkehr, verkehren	traffic/dealings, to operate
verkrüppeln	to cripple
verkutzen	to choke
verlangen	to demand
der Verlaß, verläßlich	reliance, reliable
verlassen, -ließ, -läßt	to leave, left, left
verlegen, die Verlegenheit	embarrassed, embarrassment
verletzen, die Verletzung	to injure, injury

verleumden, die Verleumdung	to defame, defamation
verlieren, verlor, verloren	to lose, lost, lost
der Verlust	loss
vermehren, die Vermehrung	to increase/to procreate, increase/procreation
vermeiden, -mieden	to avoid, avoided
vermissen, -mißte, -misst	to miss, missed, missed
das Vermögen, vermögend	wealth/assets, wealthy
vermuten	to suppose
vernichten	to wipe out
die Vernunft, vernünftig	reason, reasonable
verpassen, verpasst	to miss, missed
verpuppen	to pupate
verraten, der Verräter	to betray, traitor
verrenken	to sprain
verrückt	crazy
der Vers, Verse	verse (sg. & pl.)
die Versammlung	meeting
versäumen	to fail to do sth.
verschalen, die Verschalung	to encase, casing
verschieden, die Verschiedenheit	different, difference
der Verschleiß, verschleißen, -schliß, -schlissen	wear and tear, to wear out, wore out, worn out
verschnupft	to have a cold/rheumy
verschwenden, der Verschwender, die Verschwendung	to waste, waster, waste
verschwinden, -schwand, -schwunden	to disappear, disappeared, disappeared
das Versehen, aus Versehen	oversight, inadvertently
versöhnen, die Versöhnung	to reconcile, reconciliation
verspäten, die Verspätung	to be late/to delay, lateness/delay
das Versprechen, versprechen	promise, to promise
der Verstand, verständig	mind/reason, sensible/rational
verständigen, die Verständigung	to communicate, communication
verstauchen, die Verstauchung	to sprain, sprain
das Versteck, verstecken	hiding place, to hide
verstehen, -stand, -standen, -stehst, -steht	to understand, understood, understood, you understand, understands
der Versuch, versuchen	attempt, to attempt
verteidigen	to defend
vertilgen	to devour
der Vertrag, Verträge	contract (sg. & pl.)
vertragen, -trug, verträglich	to tolerate/to get along, tolerated/got along, agreeable/compatible
vertun, vertan	to waste, wasted (e.g. an opportunity)
verwahren, die Verwahrung	to preserve, preservation
verwaist = elternlos, verlassen	orphaned = having no parents, abandoned
verwalten, der Verwalter	to administer, administrator
verwandeln, die Verwandlung	to transform, transformation
verwandt, der Verwandte, die Verwandtschaft	related, relative, relatives
verwechseln, die Verwechslung	to mix up, mix up
der Verweis, verweisen = tadeln; -wies, -wiesen	rebuke, to rebuke = to criticize; rebuked, rebuked
verwenden, die Verwendung	to use/to apply, use/application
verwirren, verwirrt	to fluster, flustered
verwittern, die Verwitterung	to weather, weathered
verwöhnen	to spoil (a child)/to pamper
verzagen, verzagt	to lose heart, having lost heart
verzehren	to eat up
das Verzeichnis, -nisse	index (sg. & pl.)
verzeihen, -zieh, -ziehen, die Verzeihung	to forgive, forgave, forgive, forgiveness
verzichten	to renounce/to do without
verzieren, die Verzierung	to adorn, adornment
der Vetter	cousin
der Viadukt	viaduct
das Vieh, der Viehhof	livestock, corral
viel, viele, vieles	many, many, much
vielerlei, vielfach	various, multiple
vielleicht	maybe
vielmals	many times
vier, die Vier = der Vierer; vierfach, vierte, das Viertel	four, the four = the number four; fourfold, fourth, the quarter
die Viertelstunde	a quarter of an hour
vierzehn, vierzig	fourteen, forty
Viktor, Viktoria	Victor, Victoria
die Villa, Villen	villa (sg. & pl.)
violett	violet
die Violine	violin
visieren	to take aim/to gauge
die Visite	doctor's round/ward round
Vize ...., der Vizebürgermeister, Vizepräsident usw.	vice ..., the vice mayor, vice president etc.
der Vogel, Vögel	bird (sg. & pl.)

das Volk, Völker	people (sg. & pl.)
die Volksschule, Volks-schüler	elementary school, elementary school pupil
volkstümlich	folksy/vernacular
voll, völlig	full, completely
vollenden	to complete
völlig	completely
vollkommen	perfect/absolute
der Vollmond	full moon
vollständig	complete/whole
von, vom = von dem	of/from, of the/from the
voneinander	from each other
vor, vors = vor das	before, before the
voran	ahead
voraus, voraussagen	ahead/pre-, to predict/to forward/to forecast
vorbei, vorbeigehen	over/past, to go by/to pass
vorbereiten	to prepare
Vorder..., Vorderachse, Vorderfuß, Vorderrad	front..., front axle, front foot, front wheel
vordere, vorderste	front, frontmost
vorderhand = einstweilen	for the time being = in the meantime
vorerst	for now
der Vorgesetzte	superior
vorgestern	the day before yesterday
vorhanden sein	to exist/to be available
der Vorhang, -hänge	curtain (sg. & pl.)
vorher, vorherig	before, former
vorhin, im vorhinein	a little while ago, in advance
vorige, das vorige Mal	pervious, previous time
vorläufig	temporary
der Vormittag, heute vormittag, vormittags	morning, this morning, in the morning
der Vormund, -münder	guardian (sg. & pl.)
der Vorname : Taufname	first name : baptismal name/Christian name
vorn(e), von vorn(e)	at the front, start over
vornehm	distinguished/refined
der Vorrat, -räte, vorrätig	stock/provisions, stocks/provisions, in stock/available
die Vorrichtung	appliance/device
vors = vor das	before the
der Vorschlag, -schläge, vorschlagen	proposal, proposals, to suggest
die Vorsicht, vorsichtig	caution, cautious
vorstellen, die Vorstellung	to imagine, imagination
der Vorteil	advantage
der Vortrag, -träge	lecture (sg. & pl.)

vorüber	to be over
der Vorwand, -wände	pretext (sg. & pl.)
vorwärts	forward
vorzüglich	excellent
der Vulkan = feuerspei-ender Berg	volcano = fire-breathing mountain

W

die Wabe	honeycomb
wach, wachen, aufwachen	awake, to be awake, to wake up
die Wache, der Wachmann	guard, guard (male)
das Wachs, wächsern	wax, waxen
wachsam, die Wachsam-keit	watchful, watchfulness
wachsen, wuchs, ge-wachsen, du wächst	to grow, grew, grown, you grow
das Wachstum	growth
die Wacht, der Wächter	watch, watchman
wackeln, wack(e)lig	to wobble, wobbly
die Wade	calf (of a leg)
die Waffe	weapon
die Wage, wägen = abwä-gen; wog, gewogen	weighing scales, to weigh = to consider; weighed, weighed
der Wagen, die Wagen	car (sg. & pl.)
der Waggon = Eisenbahn-wagen	wagon = railroad car
der Wagner	wagon maker
waagrecht	level/horizontal
die Wahl, wählen	choice/election, to choose/to elect
der Wahnsinn, wahnsinnig	madness, mad
wahr = richtig; die Wahrheit; aber: ich war...	true = correct; truth; but: I was....
während	during
wahrhaft, wahrhaftig	truly, true
wahrnehmen, die Wahrnehmung	to perceive, perception
wahrsagen, der Wahrsager	to tell so.'s fortune, fortune-teller
wahrscheinlich, die Wahrscheinlichteit	probably, probability
die Währung	currency
die Waise = elternloses Kind	orphan = parentless child
der Wald, Wälder, waldig, die Waldung	forest/woods, forests/woods, woodsy, woodland
walken	to tumble (leather)/to full (fabric)
der Wall, Wälle	rampart/bank, ramparts/banks

wallen	to surge
die Wallfahrt, wallfahrten oder wallfahren, der Wallfahrer	pilgrimage, to go on a pilgrimage, pilgrim
Walter	Walter
die Walze, walzen, du walzt	roller, to roll sth., you roll
wälzen, du wälzt	to pore over sth., you mull over
der Walzer	waltz
die Wampe, wampig	potbelly, with a potbelly
die Wand, Wände	wall (sg. & pl.)
wandeln, verwandeln	to alter sth., to transform
wandern, der Wanderer, die Wanderung	to hike, hiker, hike
die Wandlung	transformation/transubstantiation
die Wange	cheek
wankelmütig	fickle
wanken	to stagger/to sway
wann	when
die Wanne	tub
der Wanst, Wänste	paunch (sg. & pl.)
die Wanze	bedbug
das Wappen	coat of arms
ich war, er war, wäre (von sein)	I was, he was, would be (from to be)
die Ware (des Kaufmannes)	goods (of a merchant)
warm, die Wärme, wärmen	warm, warmth, to warm
warnen, die Warnung	to warn, warning
die Warte = Ausichtsturm	observatory = watchtower
warten	to wait/to service
der Wärter	keeper
warum	why
die Warze	wart
was	what
die Wäsche, die Wäscherin, -innen	laundry, laundrywoman, laundrywomen
waschen, wusch, gewaschen, du wäschst, wäscht, das Waschbecken	to wash, washed, washed, you wash, washes, wash basin
der Wasen	vapor/steam
das Wasser, wässern, wässerig, wasserdicht	water, to water, watery, watertight
die Watsche = Ohrfeige	slap in the face = box on the ear
watscheln	to waddle
die Watte, wattieren	cotton wool, to line with wadding
weben, der Weber, der Webstuhl	to weave, weaver, loom

der Wechsel, wechseln	change, to change
der Weck oder Wecken	roll/bread roll
wecken, der Wecker	to wake, alarm clock
der Wedel, wedeln	frond, to wag
weder – noch	neither – nor
der Weg, Wegmeister	path/road, road overseer
weg = fort; geh weg!	away = off; go away!
wegbringen, weggehen usw.	to take away, to go away etc.
wegen, meinetwegen	because of, for my part
weh, weh tun	sore/aching, to hurt/to ache
wehe! wehe dir!	woe! woe betide you!
wehen, wehte, geweht	to blow, blew, blown (as in wind)
das Wehr = Mühlenwehr	dam = mill dam
wehren, sich wehren	to struggle, to defend oneself (against sth.)
das Weib, weiblich	woman/female, feminine
weich, weichen = aufweichen; weichte, geweicht	soft, to soak = to soften, softened; softened
weichen = ausweichen; wich, gewichen	to yield = to give way; yielded, yielded
weichlich	mushy/effeminate
die Weichsel	sour cherry
die Weide, weiden	pasture/willow tree, to graze
weigern	to refuse
die Weihe, weihen	consecration, to consecrate
die Weihnachten	Christmas
der Weihrauch, Weihwasser	frankincense, holy water
weil	because
die Weile, eine kleine Weile	while, a little while
der Wein, die Weinlese	wine, grape harvest
weinen, weinerlich	to weep, weepy
weiß, weißlich, weißen	white, whitish, to whitewash
weise (gescheit), die Weisen aus dem Morgenlande, die Weisheit	wise (smart), Magi, wisdom
die Weise = die Art und Weise	way = method/manner
weisen = zeigen; wies, gewiesen, du weist	to point = to show; pointed, pointed, you point
weismachen = anschwindeln; weissagen	to hoax so. = to tell a fib; to prophesy
weit, weitaus, die Weite	wide, by far, width
weiter	further
weitschichtig verwandt	distantly related
weitsichtig	farsighted
Weizen	wheat
welcher, welche, welches	which (inflected)

welk, welken	withered, to wither	(wider = gegen) aber: wieder = nochmals	(against = contrary to) but: again = once more
die Welle, wellig = gewellt	wave, wavy = rippled	der Widerhaken	barb
die Welt, der Weltteil	world, continent	der Widerhall, widerhallen	echo, to echo
wem, der Wemfall	to whom (accusative case)	widerlich	revolting
wen, der Wenfall	who/whom (accusative case)	widerspenstig	unruly
die Wendeltreppe	spiral staircase	widersprechen	to contradict
wenden, die Wendung	to turn, turn	der Widerstand, -stände	resistance (sg. & pl.)
wenig, wenige, weniges, weniger, am wenigsten	few, a few, few, fewer, fewest	widerwärtig	disagreeable/disgusting
wenigstens	at least	widerwillig	reluctant
wenn (Bindewort), wenn ... so...; in der Mundart: wann	when (conjunction), if ... then; in dialect: when	widmen	to dedicate
		wie, wieviel, wievielte, wieso	how, how many, how many/ how often, why
wer, der Werfall	who (nominative case)	wieder = nochmals	again = once more
werben, warb, geworben, du wirbst, wirbt	to advertise/to recruit, advertised/recruited, advertised/recruited, you advertize/you recruit, advertises/recruits	wiederholen, die Wiederholung	to repeat, repetition
		wiederkäuen, der Wiederkäuer	to ruminate, ruminant
		wiederkehren	to return
werden, wurde, geworden, du wirst, er wird, würde	to become, became, became, you become, he becomes, would become	wiedersehen, auf Wiedersehen	to meet again, goodbye
		wiederum	on the other hand/yet again
werfen, warf, geworfen, ich werfe, du wirfst, wirft, wirf!	to throw, threw, thrown, I throw, you throw, throws, throw!	die Wiege, wiegen = schaukeln; wiegte, gewiegt	cradle, to cradle = to rock; cradled, cradled
das Werg = Flachs, Hanf	flax tow = flax, hemp	wiegen (Gewicht), wog, gewogen	to weigh (weight), weighed, weighed
das Werk = Arbeit, Fabrik, Eisenwerk, Buch	work = labor, plant, ironworks, book	wiehern	to neigh
das Werkel	barrel organ	Wien	Vienna
die Werkstatt, -stätten, die Werkstätte	workshop, workshops, workshops	die Wiese	meadow
das Werkzeug	tool	das Wiesel	weasel
der Wert, wert, nichts wert, wertlos	value, worth, worth nothing, worthless	wieso?	why?
das Wesen	being/essence/soul	wieviel, wievielte, wievielmal	how many, how often, how many times
weshalb	why	das Wild	game (as in hunting)
die Wespe	wasp	wild, der Wilde	wild, savage
wessen, der Wesfall	whose (genitive case)	der Wilderer, wildern	poacher, to poach
der West, der Westen, nach Westen, westlich	West, West, to the west, western	der Wildfang, -fänge	captured wild animal (sg. & pl.)
die Weste	vest	wildfremd	completely strange
weswegen	why/wherefore	das Wildschwein	wild boar
die Wette, wetten	bet, to bet	Wilhelm, Wilhelmine	William, Wilhemine
das Wetter, wettern	weather, to thunder	der Wille, willig	will, willing
das Wetterleuchten	sheet lightning	Willi (von Wilhelm)	Willi (from William)
der Wettlauf, wettlaufen	race, to race	willkommen	welcome
weben, webte, gewebt	to weave, wove, woven	willkürlich	arbitrary
die Wichte, wichten	specific gravity/specific weight, to weigh sth.	wimmeln	to teem
		wimmern	to whimper
wichtig, die Wichtigkeit	important, importance	die Wimper	eyelash
wickeln, der Wickel	to swaddle, swaddle	der Wind, windig	wind, windy
der Widder (Schaf)	ram (sheep)		

WORD BOOK

die Winde, aufwinden	winch, to wind up
die Windel	diaper
winden, wand, gewunden, die Windung	to wind/to twist, wound/twisted, wound/twisted, bend/twist
windig	windy
der Wink, winken	wave/hint, to wave/to hint
der Winkel, wink(e)lig	angle/nook, angular/full of nooks and crannies
winkeln	to bend one's arm/to angle sth.
der Winter, winterlich, überwintern	winter, wintery, to over-winter
winzig klein	tiny
der Wipfel	treetop
wir	we
der Wirbel, wirbeln	whirl/eddy, to whirl
wirken, die Wirkung	to effect, effect
wirklich, die Wirklichkeit	real, reality
wirr, der Wirrwarr	confused, jumble
der Wirsing (Kohl)	savoy cabbage (cabbage)
der Wirt, die Wirtin, -innen	innkeeper, innkeeper (female), innkeepers (female)
die Wirtschaft, wirtschaftlich	economy, economic
das Wirtshaus, -häuser, die Wirtsleute	inn/tavern, inns/taverns, innkeepers
der Wisch	note/scrap of paper
wischen	to wipe
wispeln, wispern	to whisper
wissen, wußte, gewußt, ich weiß, du weißt	to know, knew, known, I know, you know
die Wissenschaft	science/scholarship
wittern	to sense/to sniff
die Witterung	weather
die Witwe, der Witwer	widow, widower
der Witz, witzig	joke, witty
wo, woanders	where, elsewhere
Woche, wochenlang	week, for weeks
wöchentlich	weekly
wodurch, wofür	through what, what for?
woher, wohin	where ... from, where to
wohl, unwohl, das Wohl	well, ill, well-being
wohl, obwohl, jawohl	possibly/arguable, although, that's right
wohlhabend	wealthy
wohlriechend	fragrant
das Wohlsein, zum Wohl-sein	well-being, for the good/to your health
die Wohltat, der Wohltäter	benefaction, benefactor
wohnen, die Wohnung	to live/to dwell, apartment/dwelling
wölben, die Wölbung	to vault, vault
der Wolf, Wölfe	wolf (sg. & pl.)
Wolfgang	Wolfgang
die Wolke, wolkenlos	cloud, cloudless
die Wolle, wollen = aus Wolle; wollene Jacke, wollig	wool, woolen = of wool; woolen jacket, woolly
wollen, wollte, gewollt, ich will, du willst	to want, wanted, wanted, I want, you want
womit	whereby
womöglich	possibly
woran	whereby
worauf, woraus	whereon, whereof
worin	wherein
das Wort, Worte u. Wörter	word (sg. & pl.)
wörtlich	literally
worüber	whereat
worunter	under which
wovon, wovor	whereof, what of
wozu	what for
der Wucher, wuchern, der Wucherer	usury, to profiteer, usurer
der Wuchs, Wüchse	growth (sg. & pl.)
die Wucht, wuchtig	vehemence, vehement
wühlen	to rummage
der Wulst, Wülste	bulge (sg. & pl.)
wund, die Wunde	sore, sore/wound
das Wunder, wunderbar	miracle, wonderful
wunderlich	peculiar
wundern, es wundert mich	to astonish, it astonishes me
der Wunsch, Wünsche, wünschen, gewünscht	wish, wishes, to wish, wished
wurde, würde (von werden)	became, would become (from to become)
die Würde, würdig	dignity, dignified
der Wurf, Würfe	throw (sg. & pl.)
der Würfel, würfeln	dice, to throw dice
würgen, erwürgen	to choke, to strangle
der Wurm, Würmer, wurmig	worm, worms, wormy
wurmen, es wurmt mich	to rankle, it rankles me
wurmstichig	wormy
die Wurst, Würste, das Würstel	sausage, sausages, small sausage
der Wurstel	fool
wursteln	to work sloppily
die Würze, würzen	spice, to spice
die Wurzel, wurzeln	root, to root

wurzen = jemanden wurzen	to exploit = to exploit so./to rip so. off
wüst	desolate
die Wüste	desert
die Wut, wüten, wütend, wütig	rage, to rage, raging, mad

X

Xavier (Name)	Xavier (name)

Y

das Ypsilon	letter y

Z

die Zacke, zackig, gezackt	sharp point/spike, pointed/jagged, serrated
zaghaft, die Zaghaftigkeit	timid, timidity
zäh, die Zähigkeit	tough, toughness
die Zahl, zählen, die Zählung	number, to count, count
zahlen, die Zahlung	to pay, payment
zahlreich	numerous
zahm, zähmen, die Zähmung	tame, to tame, taming
der Zahn, Zähne, zahnlos, das Zahnweh, Zahnrad	tooth, teeth, toothless, toothache, cogwheel
die Zange	pliers
der Zank, zanken	quarrel, to quarrel
der Zapfen, zapfen = abzapfen; das Zäpfchen	tap, to tap = to draw off; suppository
zappeln, zapp(e)lig	to fidget, fidgety
zart, zarter	delicate, more delicate
zärtlich, die Zärtlichkeit	tender, tenderness
der Zauber, zaubern, der Zauberer	magic, to do magic, magician
zaudern	to hesitate
der Zaum (Gebiß), Zäume, zäumen (Pferd)	bridle (bit), bridles, to bridle (horse)
der Zaun (Gartenzaun), Zäune, zäunen = einzäunen	fence (garden fence), fences, to fence = to fence in
zausen	to tousle
das Zebra, Zebras	zebra (sg. & pl.)
die Zeche, zechen	coal mine/check/tab, to carouse/booze
die Zecke (Tier), der Zeck	tick (animal), tick
die Zehe	toe
zehn, der Zehner, das Zehntel, zehnmal, zehnte	ten, the number ten, a tenth, ten times, tenth

das Zeichen	sign
zeichnen, die Zeichnung	to draw, drawing
zeigen, der Zeiger	to point, pointer/hand of a clock
die Zeile	line
der Zeisig	siskin
die Zeit, jederzeit, eine Zeitlang	time, anytime, for a while
zeitig, zeitlich	early, temporal
die Zeitung	newspaper
zeitweilig, zeitweise	for a time, at times
die Zelle	cell
das Zelluloid	celluloid
das Zelt	tent
das Zeltel (Buckel)	hunchback
der Zement, zementieren	cement, to cement
der Zentimeter = 1/100 m	centimeter = 1/100 meter
der Zentner = 100 kg	metric hundredweight = 100 kilograms
die Zentrale	headquarters
die Zentrifuge, zentrifugieren	centrifuge, to centrifuge
das Zentrum, die Zentren	center (sg. & pl.)
das Zepter	scepter
zer...	as prefix for nouns, expresses that something becomes something else; as prefix for nouns or verbs, expresses that one thing is being destroyed or damaged with the help of something else; as prefix for verbs, that something promising will be prevented or destroyed
die Zeremonie	ceremony
zersetzen	to disintegrate/to corrode
zerknittern	to crumple up
zerlumpt	ragged/tattered
zermalmen	to scrunch/to crush
zerreißen, -riß, -rissen	to rip, ripped, ripped
zerren, die Zerrung	to drag/to strain, strain/pulled muscle
zerstören	to destroy
zerstreuen, zerstreut, die Zerstreuung	to scatter, scattered, absent-mindedness
zerstückeln	to chop up/to break up
zertrümmern	to smash/to shatter
zerzausen	to tousle
der Zettel	slip of paper/note/leaflet
das Zeug	thing/stuff/makings of sth.

der Zeuge, zeugen	witness, to witness
das Zeugnis, -nisse	report card/certificate, report cards/certificates
die Zibebe	muscatel raisin
die Zichorie	chicory
die Ziege, Ziegenbock	goat, billy goat
der Ziegel, die Ziegelei	brick, brickworks
ziehen, zog, gezogen, ich ziehe, du ziehst, zieht, zieh! die Ziehung	to pull, pulled, pulled, I pull, you pull, pulls, pull! draw/ drawing of lots
die Ziehharmonika	accordion
das Ziel, zielen	destination/goal/aim, to aim at/to target
ziemlich	quite/considerable
zieren, die Zierde	to adorn, adornment
zierlich	delicate/petite
die Ziffer	number
die Zigarette, die Zigarre	cigarette, cigar
der Zigeuner	gypsy
das Zimmer	room/chamber
der Zimmermann, zimmern	carpenter, to carpenter
zimperlich	prissy/squeamish/pernickety
der Zimt	cinnamon
das Zink	zinc
die Zinke	tooth/prong/tine
das Zinn, verzinnen, zinnernes Geschirr	tin, to tin-coat, tin tableware
das Zins, die Zinsen, verzinsen	interest, interest, to pay interest on
der Zipfel	corner/tip/lobe
zirka = ungefähr	circa = about
der Zirkel, zirkeln	compass/circle, to circle
der Zirkus, -kusse	circus (sg. & pl.)
zirpen	to chirp
zischen	to hiss/to sizzle
die Zither	zither
die Zitrone	lemon
zittern	to shiver/to tremble
die Zitze	teat
zivilisiert	civilized
zögern	to hesitate
der Zögling	boarding pupil
der Zoll, Zölle, zollfrei	customs, customs, duty-free
der Zopf, Zöpfe	braid (sg. & pl.)
der Zorn, zornig	wrath/anger, wrathful/angry
die Zotte, die Zottel, zottig	tuft of hair, strand of shaggy hair, shaggy

zu, auf und zu	closed, open and closed
die Zucht, züchten	breed, to breed
züchtigen, die Züchtigung	to punish, punishment (physical)
das Zuchttier	breeding animal
zucken	to twitch
der Zucker, zuckern, Zuckerl	sugar, to sugar, candy
zudringlich	intrusive
zu dritt, zu zweit	in threes, in twos
zueinander	to each other/together
zuerst	at first
der Zufall, zufällig, zufälligerweise	coincidence, coincidental, by coincidence
zufrieden, die Zufriedenheit	satisfied/content, satisfaction/contentment
zu Fuß	on foot
der Zug, Züge, zugig	train/draft, trains/drafts, windy/drafty
zugänglich	approachable
der Zügel, zügeln	rein, to rein in
zugleich	at the same time
zugrunde, zugrunde gehen	basically, to perish/to go to the dogs
das Zugtier	draft animal
zu Hause	at home
zuhören	to listen
die Zukost	side dish/vegetables
die Zukunft, zukünftig	future, future
zuleide	in harm
zuletzt	last/at last
zulieb	for so.'s sake
zum = zu dem	to = to the/at = at the/in = in the/of = of the/for = for the
zunächst	first of all/initially
die Zunahme (von zunehmen)	increase/gain (from to increase)
der Zuname: Vatername	last name: father's name
zündeln	to play with fire
zünden, der Zünder, Zündholz	to light/to ignite, matches/igniter, match
der Zunder	tinder
die Zunft, Zünfte, zünftig	guild/fraternity, guilds/fraternities, proper (as in a proper meal)
die Zunge, züngeln	tongue, to flicker (as in snake or candle)
zupfen	to pluck
zur = zu der	to = to the/at = at the/in = in the/of = of the/for = for the

WITTGENSTEIN

zurecht	rightly	zwitschern	to tweet
zurück, zurückkehren	back, to turn back	zwölf, die zwölfte Stunde	twelve, the twelfth hour
zusammen	together	der Zylinder, zylindrisch.	cylinder, cylindrical.
der Zusatz, Zusätze	addition/supplement, additions/supplements		
zusehends	noticeably		
der Zustand, Zustände	state/condition, states/conditions		
zustande bringen	to bring about		
zuständig	responsible/competent		
das Zutrauen, zutraulich	trust, trusting		
zuverlässig	dependable/reliable		
zuviel	too much		
zuwege bringen	to succeed in sth./to bring sth. about		
zuwider : unangenehm	abhorrent : disagreeable		
der Zwang, zwängen	pressure/compulsion/obligation, to squeeze/to force		
zwanzig, der Zwanziger	twenty, the number twenty		
zwar	namely/whereas		
der Zweck, zwecklos	purpose/use, pointless/useless		
die Zwecke = Schuhnagel	tack/wooden peg = hobnail		
zweckmäßig	suitable/practical		
zwei, die Zwei = der Zweier, zweierlei, zweifach, zweimal, zweite, zu zweit	two, the two = the number two, two different kinds, double/two-fold, twice, second, in pairs		
zweideutig	ambiguous		
der Zweifel, zweifeln	doubt, to doubt		
der Zwerg	gnome		
die Zwetschke	plum		
der Zwickel	gusset		
zwicken	to pinch		
der Zwicker	pince-nez		
der Zwieback	zwieback		
die Zwiebel, zwiebeln	onion, to be hard on		
das Zwielicht	twilight		
das Zwiesel	forked branch		
der Zwilch	denim/drill		
der Zwilling	twin		
zwingen, zwang, gezwungen	to force, forced, forced		
der Zwinger	dungeon		
zwinkern	to wink		
der Zwirn, zwirnen	twine, to twine		
zwischen	between		

111

ABOUT THE CONTRIBUTORS

Nickolas Calabrese is an artist and writer based in Tulsa, Oklahoma.

Paul Chan is an artist based in New York. He founded the press Badlands Unlimited in 2010.

Bettina Funcke is an art historian based in New York City. She has taught and published widely, and most recently edited a book on the history of MoMA PS1. Funcke was Head of Publications for dOCUMENTA (13) and edited the *100 Notes – 100 Thoughts* book series. Her book, *Pop or Populus: Art between High and Low* was published by Sternberg Press in 2008. She is also a co-founder of the publishing collective Continuous Project and of Leopard Press.

Catherine Schelbert is a translator based in Switzerland, specializing in contemporary art, architecture and film subtitles. In 2006 she won the Prix Meret Oppenheim, Swiss Federal Office of Culture. In 2015 she was awarded the Helen and Kurt Wolff Prize from the Goethe Institute in New York for her translation of Hugo Ball's *Flametti, or The Dandyism of the Poor*.

Désirée Weber is an assistant professor in the Department of Political Science at the College of Wooster. She researches and writes about political theory and the impact of language on politics with a special focus on Ludwig Wittgenstein. She is working on a forthcoming book about the role of teaching and learning in Wittgenstein's biography and later work—and the implications for understanding our capacity to make meaning as well as judgments about meaning.